The Management of
Computer Programming
Projects

About the Author

Charles Philip Lecht, President and founder of Advanced Computer Techniques Corporation (ACT) in New York, received his start in the computer field in 1955 as a programmer for IBM. He then became a technical staff member of M.I.T.'s Lincoln Laboratory, where he worked on the systems design, analysis, and programming of the SAGE data-reduction effort. Subsequent to that he held the positions of technical staff member, The MITRE Corporation; and Chief, Programming Division, and Chief, Mobilization Application Division, Ordnance Industrial Data Agency.

Among his many professional achievements have been an election-prediction model, missile and satellite simulation models, economic models, and the systems analysis and programming of a particle-in-cell hydrodynamics model. He has been the author of many technical papers published in various scientific journals.

Mr. Lecht is the author of The Programmer's FORTRAN II and IV and The Programmer's ALGOL. Another book, The Programmer's PL/1, is soon to be published by McGraw-Hill Book Company.

In addition to writing extensively, Mr. Lecht has been very active in the academic world, teaching at such institutions as Purdue and Cooper Union. He taught in IBM's educational program at M.I.T. in addition to providing lectures on computer technology and on documentation production techniques in the United States and Europe. Mr. Lecht is also responsible for development of documentation standards in computer technology for the General Electric Company and the Monsanto Company.

Mr. Lecht has been a speaker for the American Management Association on many occasions. Also, he was chairman of the first American Management Association seminar entitled "The Management of Computer Programming Projects." Since that occasion, he has repeated the seminar several times.

The Management of Computer Programming Projects

By

CHARLES PHILIP LECHT

AMERICAN MANAGEMENT ASSOCIATION, INC.

For Jonathan Kelly Lecht,
three years old, who's just
waiting till he grows up
so he can say what he's
thinking.

Preface

The production environment of today's computer programming development project is quite different from what most nonprogramming-oriented managers think it ought to be and what many programming-oriented managers think it is. In the first case, management points to past management successes in other disciplines and feels that, somehow, similar "order" should be achievable within the programming project environment. In the second case, management suffers from an illusion that programming is a science that is as far along in its development as the technology with which it is associated--the computer. Both are wrong.

There is much illusion in the computer industry. Its personnel continually attempt to superimpose on or associate with management patterns of the past developmental environments of the present, as if this were all that were required; looking forward through a rear-view mirror.* Times have changed, and technological achievements have accelerated much more rapidly than most computer field people can comprehend.** It appears as though we have been traveling with constant speed outward along a radius on the slightly changing bottom of a bowl of infinite depth, not realizing that each unit of time that passes propels us upward more quickly and outward more slowly. We are used to change which, conversely, allows us to perpetuate our knowledge in the "plane" old way and with little or no elevation.

The desire to perpetuate past techniques in an environment which needs more is wasteful of resources. Thus, attempting to travel guided by the plain old principles of project management which once worked so well, we avoid the reality of an unfolding new dimension in project management which is required in the field of computer programming. Like Abbott's Flatland characters, we surmise the possibility of such new dimensions (failure in project enactment vis-à-vis the meeting of time and/or cost goals is widespread in today's programming environment) and are ready to accept new ideas; but alas, we can travel nowhere--for we, too, lack perception and accommodation plans.

The computer has been a technological achievement which was realized along with many others in a shorter time frame--orders of magnitude less--than any in the past for similar achievements. But the computer is a product of man, and its development a gradual extrapolation from past experience (partly since electricity and partly since the invention of the wheel) over a much longer time frame than may be established for programming, also a product of man. Indeed, programming a machine to act as man defines a sharp break with the

---

*A concept attributable first to Walt Kelly in "Pogo" and later to Marshall McLuhan, in his book The Medium Is the Massage.

**Our lower-level educational institutions saw to that. Frequently manned by "dropouts" from other college curricula, our schools tidied us up, closed our minds, and packaged us for society.

past, for prior to the late forties man had always been an integral and assumed part of the "programs" he wrote.* These few comments on the nature of and difference between machine-development technology and computer-programming technology point out, in a nutshell, why those who build the machine and those who program it should not assume that because they both are involved with it each can perform his duties according to well thought-out production techniques of the past.** Computer programming has no past (to speak of).

Now, starting with the above notions, the concept of controlling programming, making it a business enterprise within the context of procedures prepared long in the past, takes on a new dimension. For example, predicting the time and cost outcome of a moon base on the basis of uncertain know-how and the utilization of earthbound production techniques--however reliable they may be--is a difficult task at best.

One might argue that even if programming is a new discipline and the tools for controlling it are outmoded, figuring out how to do it as a business enterprise-- for example, establishing new kinds of management and production controls--is reminiscent of other challenges we have had to face and overcome in the past-- such as how to use the airplane efficiently. However, the requirement to "figure out how to do it" is more demanding this time than it has ever been, primarily because of the speed with which this must be done owing to ever increasing economic pressures. Thus today's management within computer programming is a failure-ridden lot, continually apologizing for not being able to do what they could not possibly know how to do--their failure being continually defined for them by others who haven't done it too.

Looking about the field of computer programming development, one constantly encounters time and cost overrun projects.*** This is symptomatic, because of its universality, of anything but lack of concern.**** Conferences are convened, standards are discussed, and remedies are posed which appear as realistic as the alchemist's formula for swiftly turning sand into gold. Standards in project enactment are prepared and delivered to the programming development staff, where they are laid to rest, dust-covered on bookshelves--their first chapters labeled "Enforcement"--a sad testimony to management's frustration. One might conclude that computer programming is not as well understood as many think it is and not understandable in terms of our past experience, as many think it ought to be.

---

*These were procedures to direct other men; never, significantly, machines.

**What is true of machine development is true of other disciplines "with a past"--for example, that of the fiscal controller, the assembly-line production manager, etc.

***If they are of significant size.

****Of mature management. In the case of immature (very young) management, seeming lack of concern is usually inculpable ignorance. Some people who couldn't balance their checkbooks in college control incredibly large budgets in the computer field a few years later.

Thus there are two very basic ideas, commonly held by computer people, which serve to <u>undermine</u> the establishment of worthwhile norms in programming project management: (1) Past management techniques so successful in other disciplines do not work in programming development. (2) Nothing works except a flying-by-the-seat-of-the-pants approach. The above two undermining misconceptions are unfortunately partly true; they are also partly false. It is of value to analyze them.

In the first case, the statement is true if it is taken to mean that such past techniques are <u>all</u> that is needed. However, it is false that they "do not work," for--as will be seen below and later, in the Introduction to this book--these techniques are applicable--across the board--if the manager employing them understands that more is needed.

In the second case, the statement is true if one makes his judgments <u>merely</u> through observation, since it appears as though the best managers are all "flying" that way.

Unfortunately, the two above-mentioned ideas are offensive to mature corporate management, which "sees" programming project failure as a product of management incompetence in personnel who have no time to listen. Also, and at the same time, the two ideas betray a sorry lack of thought given to solving the problems of scheduling and resource allocation by those in programming management. They, having not been met halfway by the outside world, will frequently not subscribe to anything it has to offer. Once again, both are wrong.

<u>It is the thesis of this book and the basic premise under which its author labored</u> that whatever new dimensions in project management may be required within computer programming, these will not be achieved without its management first conquering techniques of the past in such a way as to make their use automatic. This will allow for concentration on "what's new" and how to handle it. New dimensions in management are certainly needed within programming development. However, the discovery and use of these places greater demands on management. It must become accustomed to performing tasks-- proven management principles of the past--in a way that makes past management appear to have made much to-do about nothing. When this is done, new dimensions in management may be found.

This book is considered by its author to be a "first translation" of management techniques and principles commonly found in other fields into the field of computer programming. It is by no means a complete "management handbook," for much more can be said. The book avoids the presentation of theory, sticking to the presentation of procedures which have been proven to work. Where information appears sketchy, the reader should ask, prior to judging its merit, whether a more formal and well-defined description could have been given-- within the context of the <u>real</u> world of programming management. If the answer is Yes, the reader is encouraged to augment, change, etc. what is given. More on this appears in the section entitled "Guide to the Efficient Use of this Book."

This "first translation" was prepared by the author from notes, lectures, observations, etc. which he took, gave, watched, etc. However, much of the work was done by others within Advanced Computer Techniques Corporation (ACT). These associates include:

William Lone
Ralph Stout
Dorothy Walsh
Roberta Rousseau

Miss Joan Gildea did the typing of the manuscript.

Preparation of much of the material was sponsored by the Burroughs Corporation's Great Valley Laboratory, Paoli, Pennsylvania. Significant guidance and participation was acquired from members of the Programming Department at Burroughs--especially, Rankin L. Thompson, Department Manager, and William Zacharias. Some material--specifically, in the progress reporting area--was derived from work sponsored by Scientific Data Systems Incorporated, Santa Monica, California, through the offices of Essor Maso, Director of the Programming Department.

Many ideas presented in this book can be traced to the influence of D. C. Klick of the General Electric Company. These resulted from, among other professional involvements, the very successful American Management Association seminars which Mr. Klick cochaired with the author.

Finally, much tribute must be given to Maureen Kelly Lecht for encouraging the author to "Lechture on," thereby demonstrating once again her acute awareness of the current programming manager's problems.

Charles Philip Lecht

Guide to the Efficient Use of This Book

This book is intended to be used by personnel concerned with:

- Managing computer programming projects,

- Participating in computer programming projects, or simply

- Achieving an understanding of computer programming projects.

Thus its content should be of interest to those organizational elements of a corporation who are not directly engaged in computer programming development but whose responsibilities involve interaction with computer programming development groups and their management, implementation staffs, etc. The material is, however, primarily intended for computer programming development personnel at all levels.

The following is a recommended procedure for those who will use this book.

- Read the Preface.

- Read Chapter I, the Introduction, very carefully. Become familiar with the PROJECT ENACTMENT CHART included in that chapter, without worrying about precise definitions of words or items given in the chart.

- Study the Table of Contents thoroughly in order to get an idea of the book's subject matter content, organization, and structure.

- Now you are ready to study each chapter as an independent entity (except, of course, where one chapter references another). The chapters are ordered in what may be termed "natural sequence" for the given topics. This sequence generally follows the sequence of activities performed or planned for during project enactment.

- Definitions of words or word groups existing in the Glossary have been chosen for either of two reasons: Their usage is peculiar to this book, or their meaning varies widely throughout the computer industry. The Glossary is not intended to be a general dictionary of words in the computer field. Such dictionaries exist and may be obtained by the reader if desired.

- This book is intended to be "written in" by the reader. In that regard, the author desires to share authorship with whoever feels the urge to participate. The book is called in its Preface a "first translation," to drive home the point that it is deemed by the author to be a start in the establishment of a workable management system in computer programming--not an end.

- Remember that no information presented in this book can justify its reason for being a "rule" merely by its existence. Therefore, use common sense in following procedures, etc.

- Note that the PROJECT ENACTMENT CHART is certainly not intended to define a project enactment procedure for all projects. It generally describes a large development effort. This is pointed out because it is representative of much of this book's material vis-à-vis "applicability to all cases." It is expected that the reader will himself deduce the extent to which procedures need apply in any specific instance of project enactment. In short, small projects are different from large ones.

- Finally, it is important to point out that the linear representation of the sequence of project activities as shown in the PROJECT ENACTMENT CHART is not intended to be taken as literally as the form of the chart implies. Thus, for example, it is recognized that in most projects the line between end of DESIGN and beginning of CODING is not clearly defined. In fact, some DESIGN activities may persist down through to the end of the project.

- A new presentation format for display of activities which at times precede one another, at other times succeed one another, and at times occur simultaneously is needed. The chart may be most accurately interpreted as representing precedences in activity initiation times (e.g., DESIGN should start before CODING, CODING before TESTING, etc.). If taken in the context of the comments above, the chart has "more meaning." Otherwise, the reader may fall into the trap of defining the (as yet) undefinable--or worse, possibly, placing boundaries on processes which, within the current state of program implementation technology, would act to the detriment of their efficient enactment.

Table of Contents

I. Introduction

A. A REALISTIC APPRAISAL

This book presents a series of chapters the subject matter of which should be of vital interest to personnel at all levels who are directly or indirectly involved in requesting, planning, and producing computer program products. It presents guidance, techniques, procedures, standards, and other general information, all relevant to planning for, controlling, and enacting computer program development projects.

In preparing the text that follows, the author started by making as realistic an assessment as possible of the computer programming* activity--what has been learned, what may be deduced from its successes and failures in the past, observations of personnel, etc. In studying both past and present techniques in project enactment within computer programming, one cannot help but be side-tracked and awed by the enormous technical achievements which have been realized over so few years (approximately 17). These, in concert with others in the computer field--in equipment technology, usage, etc.--have collapsed concurrent and comparable achievement time frames in other fields by a great order of magnitude. In fact, such achievements in the computer field have been realized more quickly than they have in the past in any other technical discipline. Thus those involved in the development of computer hardware, software, and applications programs find themselves, at the writing of this book, in the most progressive and exciting technological field in existence today.

It is not the intent or purpose of this section to dwell on the rewarding excitement of being part of the computer field in one capacity or another. The foregoing remarks were made to point out that with the fast pace of computer programming development achievements--collapsing time frames for production of ever increasing and complex computer program products--an ever increasing need for controlling the development of these arises. The reasons for this should be clear. Changing the direction of equally large but slower-moving development efforts than those experienced in the computer field allows the imposition of lesser and more flexible demands upon management and control of product development.

---

*In this book, "computer programming" is used to include all aspects of the task of producing a computer program, including technical management, systems analysis, flowcharting, coding, testing, documenting, and performing allied clerical work. Thus the term "computer programmer" implies someone performing some or all of these tasks but always coding. The author also wishes to point out that whatever job distinctions, titles, labels, etc. are given personnel in this profession--except in the management area--the professional computer programmer can perform all of the tasks (and usually does, each to varying degrees). Thus the idea of a pure "coder" is inadmissible.

If we accept the idea that precision management is needed in order to produce larger and more complex products in shorter time spans, other interesting notions and concepts in computer programming management arise. First of all, to produce an item which is larger and more complex than was previously produced, one must either utilize more resources or increase the productivity of individuals participating in the production. One would, of course, prefer to choose the latter course of action; but doing so presupposes that personnel performance is both measurable and predictable to a greater degree than is currently indicated by experience in the computer field. Thus the usual course of action is to acquire ever increasing resources and to base estimates primarily on the addition of these, rather than on unclear, poorly defined definitions of "increased production per unit participant."

Now increasing staff presents increased problems in personnel management and control. Adding to this the very important consideration of the "type of thing" which that staff must produce--i.e., highly interdependent procedures prepared in a "foreign language" (computer programs)--implies that there must be a harmony in production equivalent to that which might be expected during the performance of a symphony orchestra. Following the analogy a bit further, the production manager may be viewed as its "conductor."*

The computer field is still very new in comparison with other fields in which comparable achievements have been realized. Computer programming has suffered insofar as the establishment or the preparation of workable procedures to conduct it goes. There are many exponents of numerous theories on how the activity can be performed with great precision. However, it is interesting to note that they themselves either are not performing or cannot perform according to the procedures which they prescribe. It is important to note that the preparation of standards in computer programming which provide the last word in how programming should be conducted cannot be achieved without understanding the nature of programming: what it is, what it produces, what personnel do, what kinds of personnel do it, etc. Achieving a "fix" on these items is not a simple task in a fast-moving environment.

What is often thought but not expressed--for whatever reason one cares to pose --is that programming, the environment in which it is done, the kind of activity which it is, the kinds of people who do it are indeed very different from anything and anyone (as a group) heretofore experienced in industry. Thus past production and management patterns are not easily extrapolatable to handle the present programming production environment. Although this point may be considered debatable, experience to date in the management and control of computer development efforts would seem to substantiate it. Then might it not be "healthier" to consider it "new" and if experiences of the past are extrapolatable, consider them a pleasant bonus?

Because of all that precedes, the author of this book is convinced that to prepare a document which is entitled "standards in something or other" and expect that title either to stick or be meaningful would be, in the most innocent

---

*This analogy and much discussion of its implications in automation has been posed by Marshall McLuhan, an expert on communications.

sense, presumptuous. Indeed, it would contribute more illusion to an industry burdened with enough of it already. This does not mean that standards should not or cannot be produced; rather, it is a warning that standards in computer programming are easy to expound upon--or even to create--but frequently are not implementable. Indeed, this very well explains why most standards books contain a chapter entitled "Enforcement." Such a chapter heading is not indicative of the natural and willing acceptance of desperately needed norms. Such books lie dusty on each programmer's bookshelf--a symbol to management of the wide abyss between theory and practice in the computer field.

This book is written in such a way as to suggest by both its form and content that its usage will be long lasting. Its guidance, techniques, procedures, and standards establish a sound foundation deemed by its author to be in keeping with the realities of what may be used today and built upon for tomorrow. Its subject matter covers 12 vital areas in computer programming project enactment, giving readers answers where the author feels they exist without attempting to impose untested theories. It starts with the concept of a project as though that item in itself were a computer program, presents a PROJECT ENACTMENT CHART (included in this chapter), and proceeds.

B. THE COMPUTER PROGRAMMING PROJECT--A DISCUSSION

What is a computer programming project? What is it for? What is its product? How is it enacted?

The above questions and many others are answered within the text of this book. Their answers arise naturally and as a byproduct of the main topics discussed in the book. It is interesting to note that since the beginning of the computer era, a very large number of computer program development projects have been performed in a wide variety of circumstances producing a wide variety of products. Yet there is no general agreement upon the meaning of the word "project" within the computer programming field.

Scores of projects have been and continue to be performed within computer-manufacturer organizations and computer-user facilities where neither management nor the staff involved in project performance have a clear understanding of what they should be doing to insure success, what they should be doing to prevent project failure, and what they should not be doing. Nonetheless, projects do get started and do end, and products are produced. One may then deduce that those involved in both the management and technical-implementation activities must be doing something right. But to do "something" right is not enough.

Ever increasing cost expenditures resulting either directly or indirectly from the planning for and/or enactment of computer programming development projects are a major concern of cost-conscious management in every company in which these projects take place. In addition, there is a problem in the lack of definition of precisely what a computer programming project entails in the minds of management responsible for but not directly involved in computer programming development work. Thus it is interesting that very frequently:

1. Projects fail to meet reasonable objectives.

2. Projects fail to meet unreasonable objectives supposed to be reasonable (meeting reasonable ones in the process but no one knows it).

3. Projects fail to meet reasonable objectives but are termed successes (by changing the original objectives at the completion of the project).

True, some projects do succeed in meeting their objectives and are judged successes upon completion; however, the frequency of occurrence of such projects is woefully low within the computer field. Indeed, the preponderance of projects in the computer programming field reside in categories 1, 2, and 3 indicated above. Each categorized as "having failed to meet its objectives" is, however, radically different from the others.

The number of projects in the first category can be reduced by increasing technical competency on the part of the production staff. The number of projects in the second category can be reduced by increased competency on the part of the managerial staff. The third category bears no comment. Whatever the case, the cornerstone of planning for and performing a successful computer programming project rests in a common understanding by all concerned of a computer programming project and how it is enacted.

Note the PROJECT ENACTMENT CHART at the end of this chapter.* It represents all major activities performed by programming development personnel from receipt of a work order (EXTERNAL FUNCTIONAL SPECIFICATION) through delivery of a product and its entry into MAINTENANCE. It will be seen in Chapter III, "Time and Cost Estimating," that the PROJECT ENACTMENT CHART actually represents two projects rather than one. Indeed, this concept is vital to the establishment of meaningful time and cost estimates for product development. The two may be described as follows:

Type 1: A research project during which the work order is analyzed (ANALYSIS), its definition formalized, a plan of production established, and the results reviewed (ALPHA REVIEW).

Type 2: An implementation project starting (DESIGN) with the output of Type 1 above (PROGRAMMING FUNCTIONAL SPECIFICATIONS and a WORK PLAN) and ending with a quality test (ACCEPTANCE REVIEW).

The activities of CUSTOMER ACCEPTANCE PERIOD support and MAINTENANCE are included on the chart for completeness.

One great error made repeatedly by programming people is failure to distinguish between project Types 1 and 2, above, when rendering estimates of time, cost, resources, etc. to their management. Because of this, it is frequently the case that the DESIGN phase is entered--implementation--under the shadow

---

*Its key is on the second page of the chart.

of lateness, cost overruns, and all the other unhappy results of having missed prespecified goals before the action was even started. As will be seen in Chapter III--"Time and Cost Estimating"--and Chapter II--"Work Plan Preparation"--you cannot reasonably expect to provide a meaningful estimate of anything without knowing what the estimates are for (PROGRAMMING FUNCTIONAL SPECIFICATIONS) and how you intend to do the work (WORK PLAN).

Equally responsible for the initiation of project Type 2 with predefined failure (as discussed above) is management that insists upon having fixed commitments from programming personnel prior to the latter's understanding what the commitments are for. Too frequently, management does not realize that in asking the staff for "the impossible," the staff will feel the obligation to respond out of respect, fear, or misguided loyalty. Saying "no" to the boss frequently requires courage, political and psychological wisdom, and business maturity that comes with much experience. Other conditions for predefined failure exist, but it is not the purpose of this chapter to delve into them--e.g., the belief that everything is programmable, preoccupation with techniques to the exclusion of sound business judgment, etc.

Thus it is important that both management--at all levels--and programming personnel understand the process by which an implementation project starts-- the activities up to DESIGN on the project chart. Also, and of great importance, should be the concurrent desire of both groups jointly to insure fulfillment of the research and development project objectives as quickly as possible so that implementation may be launched if the CONFORMANCE REPORT of the ALPHA REVIEW committee is in the affirmative.

From here on in this book, the word "project" will always refer to Type 2 as defined above unless otherwise noted. (Also, the descriptions "Type 1" and "Type 2" are not used again.) The PROJECT ENACTMENT CHART shows a "paper flow" associated with a sequence of major events. This "paper flow" is thoroughly covered in the book in Chapter IV, entitled "Specification Reviews." It is interesting to note how much of the programmer's job involves writing other than computer code (see CHART A at the end of this chapter under the heading PROJECT ENACTMENT TIME SCALES AND MEASURES). The average programmer spends approximately 20 percent of his time in this way.

More comments are in order concerning the subject chart. One very important observation is that its form gives the impression that all activities follow a well-defined time sequence. There are three major reasons--and many minor ones--why this is not true in actual project enactment.

MAJOR REASONS

- No matter how well defined the product to be developed is at the start of a project, much will be learned during implementation.

- Resources are costly enough and the efficiency with which the resources may be used sufficiently less than ideal to make overlap desirable.

- Putting together a program system requires "conducting" the staff as a group to harmonize their production checkpoint achievements (see Chapter V, "Project Enactment Checkpoints").

Thus whether it is one program or a program system, produced by one programmer or a group of programmers, no well-defined and consistent time sequence is to be presupposed in today's production environment. Notwithstanding this fact, there is a "not so well defined" time sequence of events in product development. It is best represented by CHART B under the heading PROJECT ENACTMENT TIME SCALES AND MEASURES, at the conclusion of this chapter. This chart views the activities of one programmer producing one program from DESIGN through DEBUG. On this chart it may be observed that each programmer cannot <u>initiate</u> certain activities without predecessor activities having been <u>initiated</u>. Thus in normal circumstances initiation of coding should not take place prior to initiation of flowcharting, initiation of debugging may not take place prior to initiation of coding, etc. Note that at the end of the single programmer's single-program project, he is probably doing all activities in a "time shared" manner. Extrapolate this to many programmers working upon many programs all to be integrated into one system; consider the management problem; and the analogy of "conducting a symphony" once again quite naturally arises. Gone are the time-sequenced production line techniques of the past, and born is the concept of organic creation and integration in a harmonizing environment.

How much "harmony" can be achieved is the question. The key to obtaining maximum harmony during production is found in the study of project enactment techniques, which regulate the activities of the project enactment team individually and in concert.

Tried and true past management techniques need not be abandoned in the programming project enactment environment.* Indeed, WORK PLAN PREPARATION, TIME AND COST ESTIMATING, PROGRESS REPORTING, SPECIFICATION REVIEWS, etc. still work. Thus if the technical programming manager is to be able to devote proper time to "creating the organic harmony" of his production effort, producing these must become a routine, matter-of-fact activity in the project enactment environment.

This book presents, in addition to other information, the plans and procedures for handling the matter-of-fact (discussed above) activity performance requirements within any programming organization.

---

*Such abandonment by technical personnel who functioned well in other production environments is usually the result of unhappiness with their inability to time-sequence events in the programming environment with great precision.

PROJECT CHARTS:

PROJECT ENACTMENT TIME SCALES AND MEASURES

PROJECT ENACTMENT CHART

PROJECT ENACTMENT TIME
SCALES AND MEASURES

These charts provide a graphic representation of two items:

CHART A: Shows average activity times which may be expected to occur per computer programmer assigned a single program* to design, code, debug, and document.** Also, as will be seen on the chart, some time in pure clerical work is required. No time spent in integration and systems test is allowed for. The statistics given are derived from the study of the performance of twenty programmers over a period of two years, coding in assembly and compiler languages for a large computer system.

CHART B: Shows a simplified model of a single programmer's time-sequenced activity initiations in developing a single program. This model is simplified--i.e., does not show all the activities given in the PROJECT ENACTMENT CHART --to emphasize the initiation times and overlap of major activities.

---

*Program is used here to mean a "programming assignment," which may be a subprogram, module, piece of a larger program, etc.

**Draft documentation to be given to the technical writing staff. Also includes preparation of progress reports.

CHART A: THE PROGRAMMER'S TIME

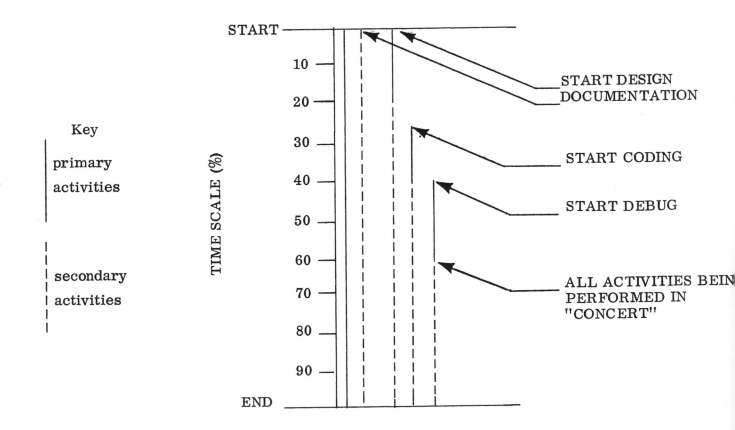

DESIGN 30%

DOCUMENT 18%

CODE 20%

DEBUG 30%

CLERICAL 2%

CHART B: MODEL OF MAJOR ACTIVITY INITIATION TIMES FOR ONE PROGRAM WORKED UPON BY ONE PROGRAMMER

Key

| primary activities

¦ secondary activities

TIME SCALE (%)

START
10
20
30
40
50
60
70
80
90
END

START DESIGN DOCUMENTATION

START CODING

START DEBUG

ALL ACTIVITIES BEIN PERFORMED IN "CONCERT"

PROJECT ENACTMENT CHART

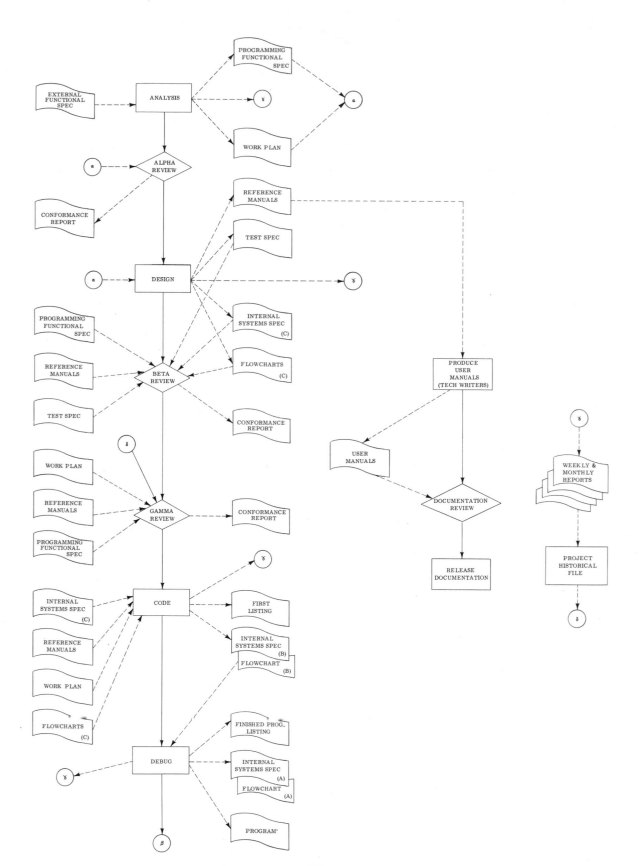

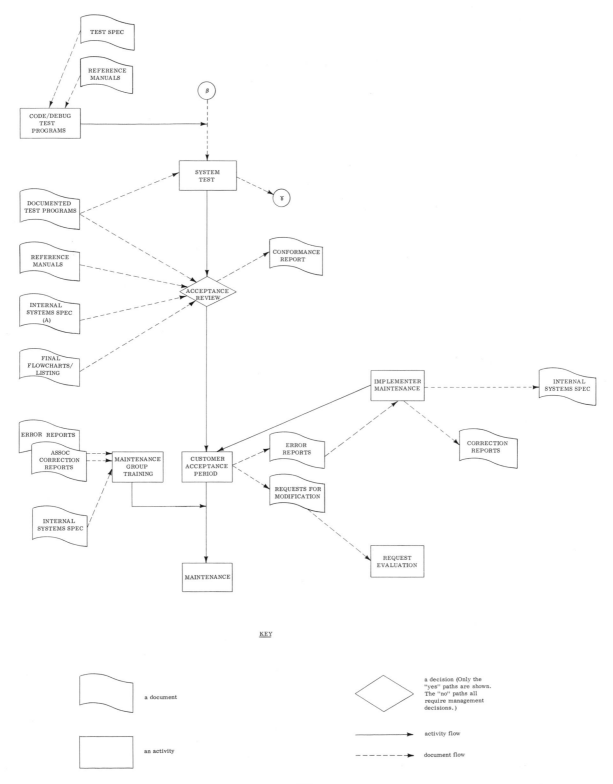

TEST SPEC

REFERENCE
MANUALS

CODE/DEBUG
TEST
PROGRAMS

β

SYSTEM
TEST

ƴ

DOCUMENTED
TEST PROGRAMS

REFERENCE
MANUALS

INTERNAL
SYSTEMS SPEC
(A)

FINAL
FLOWCHARTS/
LISTING

ACCEPTANCE
REVIEW

CONFORMANCE
REPORT

IMPLEMENTER
MAINTENANCE

INTERNAL
SYSTEMS SPEC

ERROR REPORTS

ASSOC
CORRECTION
REPORTS

MAINTENANCE
GROUP
TRAINING

CUSTOMER
ACCEPTANCE
PERIOD

ERROR
REPORTS

CORRECTION
REPORTS

REQUESTS FOR
MODIFICATION

INTERNAL
SYSTEMS SPEC

REQUEST
EVALUATION

MAINTENANCE

KEY

a document

an activity

a decision (Only the
"yes" paths are shown.
The "no" paths all
require management
decisions.)

activity flow

document flow

29

NOTES

II. Work Plan Preparation

A. INTRODUCTION

Failure means not living up to expectation. In an industry accustomed to the imposition of unrealistic goals--and therefore predefined failure--the need for accurate planning documentation and the means for producing it is apparent.

The purpose of this chapter is to specify the minimum content of an adequate WORK PLAN and to describe in the context of overall project enactment a process by which a high level of realism can be attained in its production.

Beginning with a request for a specific product, the programming manager starts the ANALYSIS PHASE--i.e., that period of development during which a programming project leader and his staff* examine the problem and put into writing their interpretation of the task to be performed. Two documents are generated--a WORK PLAN and a PROGRAMMING FUNCTIONAL SPECIFICATION.

The latter is a restatement of the EXTERNAL FUNCTIONAL SPECIFICATION in technical language, following the preliminary period of study. The former is to be the subject of this chapter.

Prior to presenting the details of this chapter, it is important to note that preparing the WORK PLAN heavily involves estimation of resources (as will be seen in the following sections). The chapter entitled "Time and Cost Estimating"--which spells out, among many other things, how to prepare a formal estimate--will utilize many of the deductions to be made during WORK PLAN preparation. Thus this chapter and the "Time and Cost Estimating" chapter are complementary vis-à-vis the preparation of formal estimates, and this is as it should be. The reader may wish to review both prior to using either.

WORK PLAN preparation begins with an analysis of the task to be performed.

B. HOW TO PREPARE THE WORK PLAN

1. Analyze the task.

   The following activities must take place prior to estimating:

   ● An EXTERNAL FUNCTIONAL SPECIFICATION must have been received.

   ● The EXTERNAL FUNCTIONAL SPECIFICATION must have been studied in the DESIGN phase, and from it a PRELIMINARY PROGRAMMING FUNCTIONAL SPECIFICATION must have been developed.

---

*The staff used during this phase should be of a high experience level. It will form the technical core of the effort should the work be continued beyond the ALPHA review. For this reason more competency will be assumed of the staff members during the ANALYSIS PHASE than in subsequent stages of the project enactment.

Now the following three questions are asked.

Q_1 WHAT IS THE TASK?

It is important to divide the task into recognizable <u>elements</u>. These elements will involve computer programs, as well as other activities which must be performed. The principle here is that the task is to be segmented into small items or elements against which resources may be placed.

For example, assume the project consists of the development of a computer program package such as a critical path method (CPM) model. Then the answer to question Q_1 might be given as follows:

- The input module.
- The calculation module.
- The output module.
- The dating module.
- The updating module.
- Preparation of test cases.
- Integration of CPM modules.
- Preparation of a user's manual.
- Preparation of an internal systems manual.
- Attendance at project meetings.

Chart 1-A, described in Supplement 1 of this section, should be filled out.

Q_2 WHO WILL PERFORM THE WORK?

Because programming is a highly people-dependent activity, the most accurate estimates can be made only when each element (specified in 1, above, "Analyzing the Task") of the system can be associated with the person(s) who will perform the work. Thus in answering this question, names are associated with the task elements, if at all possible.*

Now prepare Chart 1-B, Supplement 1.

Q_3 IS THE LOGISTICAL SUPPORT AVAILABLE?

Support items are necessary to a computer programming project. State the availability of:

- A computer.
- Office space.
- Supplies.
- Etc.

---

*If not all names are available (or essential according to the judgment of the manager preparing the WORK PLAN), key names should exist. As will be seen, accuracy in estimating declines rapidly as the number of missing names increases.

List these items very carefully in Chart 1-C.

2. Develop time estimates.

    The following procedures are used for estimating the project development time per element.

    ● Isolate tasks.

        The form for Chart 2, Supplement 1, should be prepared first. This is a bar chart, which has along its vertical axis the names per element of the personnel who will work on the project and along its horizontal axis, time.

        It is important that this chart be carefully developed (although it will be discarded later on in the estimating process). Without a careful rendition of what this chart is to look like, the estimator cannot achieve a solid view of the maximum personnel requirement for the job.

    ● Consult HISTORICAL FILES.

        Associated with every project enacted at many companies is a PROJECT HISTORICAL FILE. This consists of a PROJECT HISTORICAL RECORD (see PROGRESS REPORTING) plus weekly and monthly reports.

        Scan the records of similar projects or of projects having some similar subset of tasks--if there are any--in order to get a feel for the situation. If progress in some area occurred in an unusual way, consult the WEEKLY REPORTS for the appropriate project weeks; an explanation should be provided in the REMARKS section.

        Reconstruct a "normal" version of that PROJECT HISTORICAL RECORD, eliminating all delays that could be attributed to the unexpected.

        After several such reconstructions have been made, averaging methods (see PROGRESS REPORTING) can be used to derive an expected progress record.

    ● Review estimate with personnel.

        The estimator calls each individual into his office to discuss the project element(s) with which that individual is expected to be concerned. There are, of course, other ways in which the feedback from the prospective participant can be achieved; however, the best way is through direct review of the work to be done, as if in negotiation.

        The estimator should judge each project element as though he were going to do the job himself. He should then ask the proposed project personnel for their view of the work to be performed.

        If he knows the individual, so much the better. Whether he does or does not, he must discuss each element of the project until coming to a time decision.

This is the most crucial activity in time estimating. There is no substitute for it. The estimator should be sufficiently knowledgeable to understand the work and also to understand the proposed participant's possible reactions to it. If the estimator does not have these capabilities, he is "licked" at the start.

Each person should be brought in, queried, and the length of time for completion of his task established.

Chart 2, Supplement 1, will then show the length of time that both the estimator and the proposed participants decided upon as being reasonable for the elements of the project.

3. Develop the PROJECT NETWORK.

A PROJECT NETWORK is a PERT DIAGRAM showing the developmental relationships between all logical components of the system. This should show which tasks must precede others during enactment.

4. Develop the staffing pattern.

Using the PROJECT NETWORK, the estimator should develop Chart 3, Supplement 1, taking care that personnel are not removed too readily from their respective work assignments.*

Chart 3 optimizes the personnel assignments in time.

5. Develop the computer time requirement.

From discussions with the staff and from personal experience it is possible to infer for each program to be developed:

t_d: The duration of expected computer usage.**

Δt: An arbitrary time increment to be used in calculating the computer time requirement (usually a day, week, or month).

m: The maximum hourly requirement per Δt.

Using these parameters, Chart 4, Supplement 1, can be developed.

Chart 4 is a bell shaped curve having a maximum height equal to m, spread over a width equal to the duration of checkout t_d for the module.

By "integrating" the curve, one can arrive at an estimate of computer time requirements. This can best be done by subdividing t_d into n equal units

---

*At the completion of a particular program segment there is usually a maintenance period, as well as an education period for new users.

**Usually about 30 percent of the development time for any single module.

34

(each of width $\underline{\Delta t}$) and by projecting a vertical line from the midpoint of each interval to the curve, noting the intersection.

To each intersection there corresponds a time interval in hours. By reading off all such values and summing them, the time required for debugging a single program can be computed.

SYSTEM TESTING usually does not conform to the bell-shaped curve model described above. Experience has shown that this phase of testing requires a constant block of time daily.

The total time needed is the sum of the debugging and system test requirements (see Chart 5, Supplement 1).

Each component of the system has its anticipated test duration.

Chart 5 is an example of the derivation of maximum daily computer time requirement. A chart is prepared including one bell-shaped curve for every system module, placed according to its anticipated test duration. By summing these curves, another curve--the maximum $\underline{\Delta t}$ requirement--can be plotted.

Compare the maximum daily computer time requirement with resources available.

If known resources are exceeded, two courses are possible--an expansion of computer time allocation to the project or a schedule revision.

C. FORMAT OF THE WORK PLAN

Appendix 1, "How to Use the Model Reports," gives the format of the WORK PLAN.

D. WORK PLAN MAINTENANCE

The PROJECT WORK PLAN is initially used to help in developing a formal time and cost estimate. Its subsequent use is as an aid in project management, control, etc.

If (or as) changes occur during project enactment, the WORK PLAN must be amended to reflect them. The process of amending the WORK PLAN is called WORK PLAN MAINTENANCE. Thus the original version of the WORK PLAN plus its amendments constitutes a historical record of project goals, estimates, plans, etc.

The uses of such a historical record, over and above its use for management meetings, should be obvious.

WORK PLAN PREPARATION

SUPPLEMENT 1

The following charts are prepared during WORK PLAN PREPARATION.

CHART 1

Chart 1 can be prepared only after the task has been segmented into logical sections; this implies some knowledge of the system.

- Chart 1-A lists logical components (element names) and indicates whether each subtask is known or unknown at the outset.

- Chart 1-B lists component names versus personnel. If the person who will develop the element is known, his name is listed opposite the element name under KNOWN. Otherwise, an X appears in the UNKNOWN column.

- Chart 1-C is a list of required resources. Opposite each entry is an indication of whether the support is known to be available or not.

To the author of the WORK PLAN any X in the NOT KNOWN column indicates that fixed time and personnel estimates cannot be given and that the supporting DISCUSSION for the plan must detail the areas of uncertainty; to the author of the TIME AND COST ESTIMATE any X in the NOT KNOWN column implies a T&M--not an FCFT estimate.*

CHART 2

Chart 2 is a personnel-time per element bar chart. Along the horizontal axis are listed the names of all system components and the employee names associated with each. The time required for an employee is represented by a bar in the chart.

In the sample which follows, the elements of the hypothetical system are listed as $ELEMENT_1$, $ELEMENT_2$, ... $ELEMENT_n$. Employee names are replaced by letters--i.e., $N_1, N_2, N_3, ...$; $N_1, N_2, N_3, ...$; etc.

Chart 2 is valuable in indicating the maximum number of personnel required at any one time for the project.

CHART 3

Chart 3 is a reorganization of Chart 2. In the sample the same conventions are used to represent element and employee names.

---

*Unless a calculated risk is desired.

The difference between Charts 2 and 3 is that Chart 3 depicts the actual arrangement of activities in time, as defined in the PERT DIAGRAM; Chart 2 simply is a time estimate for each module of the system, in time dependencies being considered.

CHART 4

Chart 4 is a bell-shaped curve used in the development of computer time estimates for individual portions of the system.

The m is the maximum number of hours per day required at peak testing time.

The t_d is the duration of the CHECKOUT phase for the module being estimated.

The curve is drawn as follows:

- Subdivide t_d into thirds.

- The intersection of the second third with the dotted line representing m will be the "top" of the curve (see sample diagram).

- Testing will begin using only a minimum amount of time--possibly the time for a single compilation--and will end at a similar level. Note this minimum requirement twice ($t=0$ and $t=t_d$) on the diagram.

- Connect the three points so derived with a smooth bell-shaped curve which rises gradually until two-thirds of the proposed duration of testing has taken place (see sample Chart 4).

CHART 5

Many system components will be tested simultaneously. Once the individual estimates are made, a summation chart--Chart 5--can be developed.

Chart 5 is intended primarily to assure that the maximum daily computer time requirement for the entire project does not exceed the maximum daily allocation.

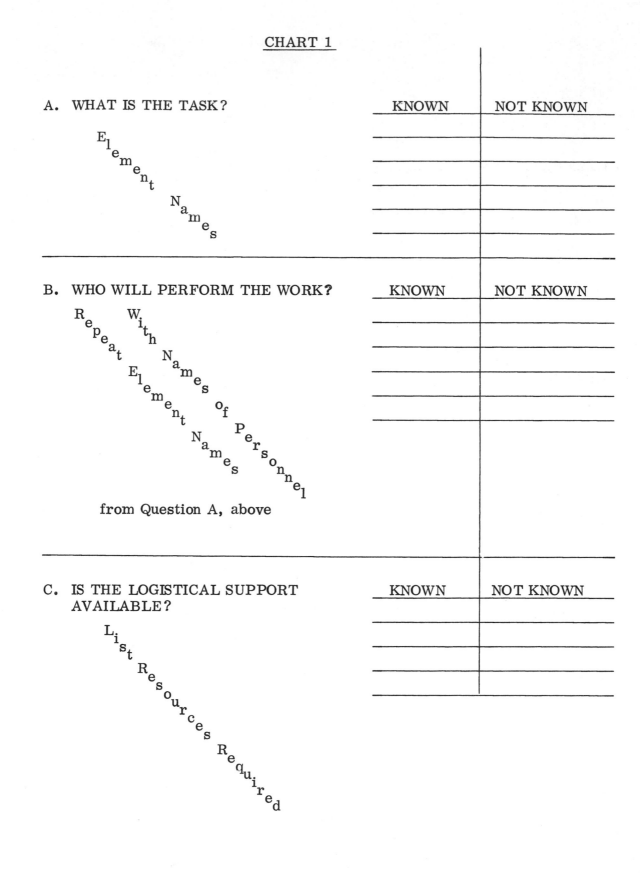

CHART 1

A. WHAT IS THE TASK?   KNOWN   NOT KNOWN

Element Names

B. WHO WILL PERFORM THE WORK?   KNOWN   NOT KNOWN

Repeat With Names of Personnel Element Names

from Question A, above

C. IS THE LOGISTICAL SUPPORT AVAILABLE?   KNOWN   NOT KNOWN

List Resources Required

38

CHART 2

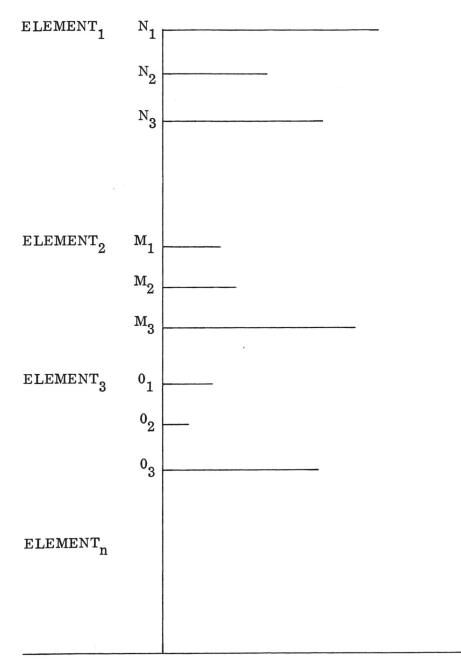

STAFF
PER ELEMENT

ELEMENT$_1$ N$_1$

N$_2$

N$_3$

ELEMENT$_2$ M$_1$

M$_2$

M$_3$

ELEMENT$_3$ 0$_1$

0$_2$

0$_3$

ELEMENT$_n$

TIME

CHART 3

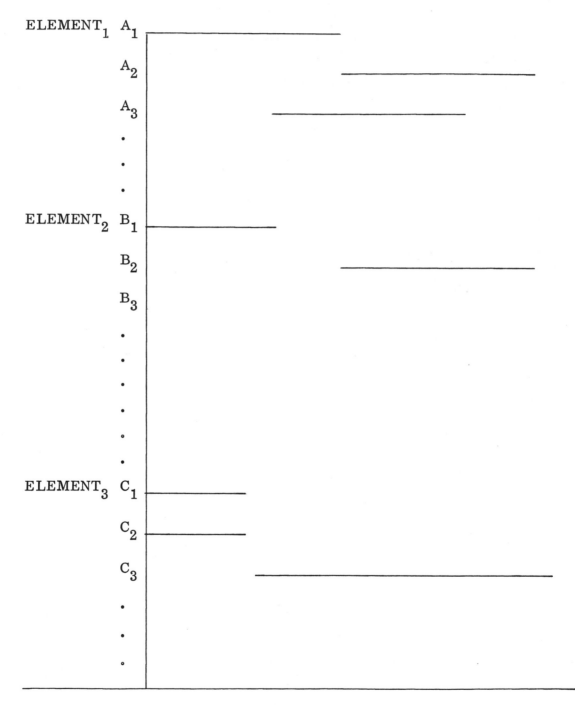

STAFF
PER ELEMENT

ELEMENT$_1$ A$_1$

A$_2$

A$_3$

.

.

.

ELEMENT$_2$ B$_1$

B$_2$

B$_3$

.

.

.

.

.

.

ELEMENT$_3$ C$_1$

C$_2$

C$_3$

.

.

.

TIME

CHART 4

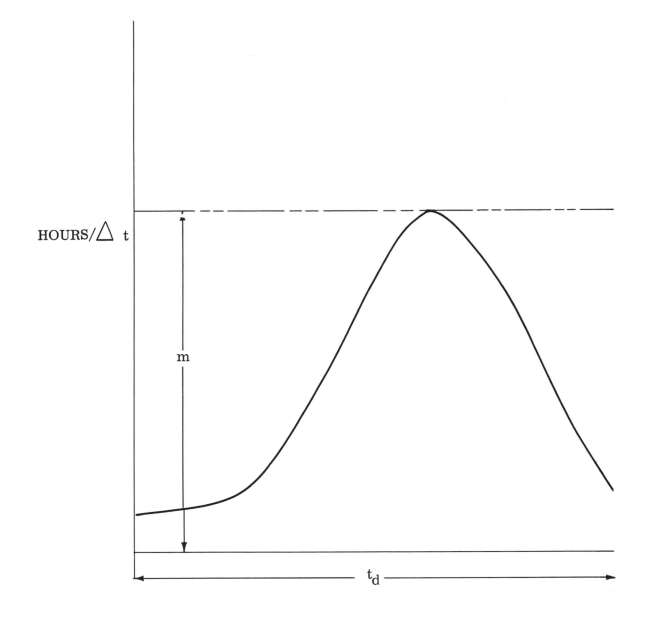

Bell-shaped curve used to compute machine requirement for
a system component

CHART 5

Example of derivation of maximum daily requirements -- C_1 denotes the ith component of the system.

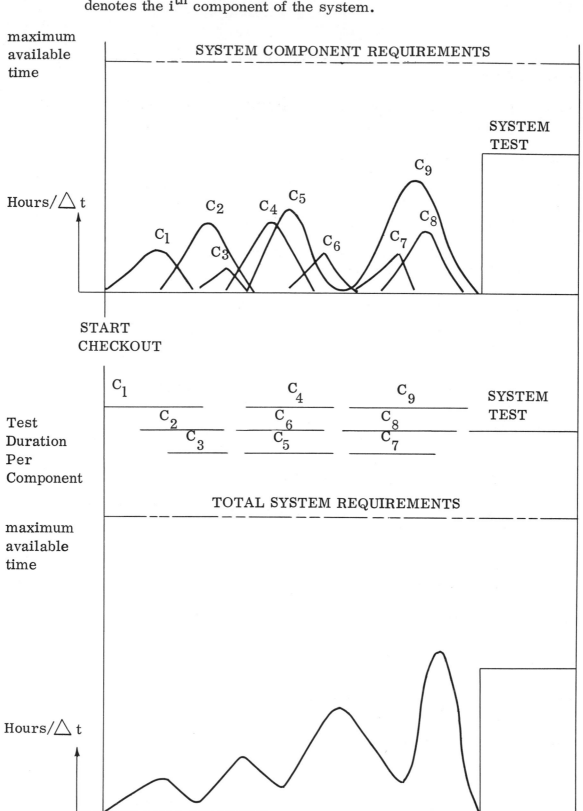

CHECKLIST FOR
WORK PLAN PREPARATION

	YES	NO
Has an EXTERNAL FUNCTIONAL SPECIFICATION been received?	☐	☐
Does a PROGRAMMING FUNCTIONAL SPECIFICATION exist?	☐	☐
Is the task well defined?	☐	☐
Has sufficient ANALYSIS taken place to enable the system to be subdivided into a set of component parts?	☐	☐
● If a subdivision exists, is it sufficiently fine for estimating purposes?	☐	☐

> A DETAILED BREAKDOWN OF THE SYSTEM
> GREATLY REDUCES THE ESTIMATING TASK.

	YES	NO
● Does each set unit have a precise functional definition?	☐	☐
● Has Chart 1-A been completed?	☐	☐

> IF UNKNOWNS ARE INDICATED IN CHART 1,
> THE WRITER MUST STATE THAT NO FCFT
> ESTIMATE CAN BE BASED ON THIS WORK PLAN.

	YES	NO
● Can a programmer's name be associated with every system component?	☐	☐
● Has Chart 1-B been completed?	☐	☐
Are all relevant PROJECT HISTORICAL RECORDS available?	☐	☐
Are the needed support items known?	☐	☐
Has Chart 1-C been completed?	☐	☐

	YES	NO
Has a first estimate for each system component been made, on the basis of FUNCTIONAL SPECIFICATIONS and PROJECT HISTORICAL RECORDS?	☐	☐
Have these estimates been discussed with personnel, and have revised estimates been decided upon?	☐	☐
Has Chart 2 been completed?	☐	☐
Has a PROJECT NETWORK been developed?	☐	☐
Has Chart 3 been completed?	☐	☐
Has the computer time requirement been derived?	☐	☐
• Was computer time discussed with the individual staff members?	☐	☐
• Was each asked to estimate his maximum daily requirement in hours?	☐	☐
• Was Chart 4 developed for each system component?	☐	☐
• Was Chart 5 drawn to estimate the maximum daily requirement for the entire project?	☐	☐

> OFTEN, ESTIMATORS IGNORE THE FACT THAT THERE IS A LIMIT TO THE COMPUTER TIME AVAILABLE IN A DAY. THIS LIMIT AS WELL AS THE MAXIMUM TIME NEED ARE PLOTTED IN CHART 5. EXCEEDING THE LIMIT IMPLIES EITHER INCREASED TIME ALLOCATION OR A SCHEDULE REVISION.

	YES	NO
Has a complete DISCUSSION section been included in the WORK PLAN?	☐	☐
• If some items necessary to accurate estimating are missing at this time, have they been mentioned?	☐	☐
• Have supporting documents (Charts 1 through 5, etc.) been supplied, to emphasize any missing information?	☐	☐

NOTES

NOTES

III. Time and Cost Estimating

A. INTRODUCTION

It is frequently said that estimating the time and/or cost of a computer programming project is an almost impossible task. When discussing estimating in other disciplines--e.g., engineering--personnel are far more inclined to "put themselves on the line," launching into the job of preparing estimates with confidence. Programming managers point out that the number of uncertainties with which they must contend plus the lack of standards in their field serves to preclude the possibility of estimating with confidence; there is widespread reluctance in regard to the preparation of formal estimates.

Some personnel, in fact, feel that completing an estimate can be hazardous to their careers. Their reluctance is born of the following experiences:

- Past time and cost estimating results have been catastrophic.

- The rapidity with which many programming projects change makes the task of estimating a frustrating exercise.

- Computer programming is, at this point in time, so heavily dependent upon the people involved that estimating seems to defy the establishment of any rule of thumb.

- It has been found that any attempt at maintaining a reasonable schedule will be frustrated if a high degree of reliability within the computer facility cannot be achieved.

Many other reasons may be proposed. It can be seen, however, that whatever the reason, most personnel beg the question as to what to do even in a case where ideal conditions exist.

The estimator should be aware of six axioms:

- Time and cost estimates of programming projects are of vital necessity to management.

- All estimates must proceed from a concept of the project as performed under ideal conditions.

- The estimator's judgment of unknowns affecting his estimate should be taken into account only after the ideal-conditions estimate has been prepared.

- The preparation of an estimate is an iterative procedure and cannot be performed once and for all at the first attempt.

- A partial estimate is better than none.

- Estimates should be considered independently of the task of adhering to schedules.

It should be clear that every estimate is necessarily based on the experience and judgment of its author, whether it be in computer programming or in any other field. Some items influencing the estimate are so well understood that judgment seems to be replaced by the mere mechanical application of a rule, while others depend heavily upon the experience of the estimator.

It is true that computer programming is a relatively new profession. It is true that as an activity to be time-and-cost estimated within a business environment it is even newer--approximately ten years old. It is also true that because of its "newness" as a technical activity to be performed in conjunction with other activities which are much better understood and for which much experience exists, the frequency of change in the scope, content, etc. is relatively high. Nonetheless, much experience has been gained over the past ten years to allow for the development of computer programming estimates based on an ideal programming environment for the context in which the estimate is made. Methodologies have been formulated to develop these estimates for actual project requirements.

The proposition that time and cost estimating in computer programming is an impossible task reflects, more than anything else, the frustration of attempting to adhere to estimates despite project fluctuations.

The approach to time and cost estimating to be used in this chapter will be based on the project definition and segmentation provided by the PROJECT WORK PLAN.

In order to clarify concepts at the start, it is necessary to state that the cost and/or the expenditure of time is caused by the utilization of resources to perform a task and not by the task itself. This simple thought is stated to indicate that when the elements of a project to be time-and-cost estimated are discussed:

- Some will be directly translatable into funds--e.g., computer time.

- Others will require a multiple translation--e.g., designing a specific system component entails viewing it first as a computer program, then as an activity to be performed by someone within a specific period of time, and finally, in terms of the cost of that "someone."

B. THE DEFINITION OF A COMPUTER PROGRAMMING PROJECT

A computer programming project:

- Is an activity which has a defined START-POINT.

- Is an activity which has a defined END-POINT--i.e., a definition of completion.

- Has a known ACTIVITY TO BE PERFORMED.

1. The project START-POINT.

    Opinion varies as to the definition of the project START-POINT. Some
    hold that a project starts as soon as an order for the item is received,
    even prior to preparation of the first formal definition* of the item.
    Others say that the computer programming project does not start until
    the formal statement has been prepared.

    It is supposed that the organization originating a computer programming
    project will present development personnel with an EXTERNAL FUNC-
    TIONAL SPECIFICATION.

    There is a period of time between the point at which the computer pro-
    gramming development group receives the EXTERNAL FUNCTIONAL
    SPECIFICATION and their decision that they can fulfill its requirements.
    This period is spent in review of the submitted material. On the PROJECT
    ENACTMENT flowchart this is shown as the ANALYSIS PHASE. Note
    that the product of this phase is the PROGRAMMING FUNCTIONAL
    SPECIFICATION and a PROJECT WORK PLAN.

    The computer programming project will <u>not</u> be said to start upon the re-
    ceipt of an EXTERNAL FUNCTIONAL SPECIFICATION. There can be
    no certainty in the amount of time to be spent studying it and producing
    the PROGRAMMING FUNCTIONAL SPECIFICATION and the PROJECT
    WORK PLAN. No reasonable development time and cost estimating can
    be done without these documents existing. They define the job to be
    done.

    This book defines the project START-POINT as the beginning of DESIGN.**

2. The project END-POINT.

    The definition of a project includes the definition of a project END-POINT.

    The project END-POINT is defined by a formal statement of the criteria
    by which the project will be judged to have been completed. Examples of
    this can be:

    - A list of objectives to be achieved.

    - Specifications to be met.

---

*EXTERNAL FUNCTIONAL SPECIFICATION--See the PROJECT ENACT-
MENT flowchart, Chapter 1.

**The ANALYSIS PHASE, occurring between receipt of the EXTERNAL
FUNCTIONAL SPECIFICATION and production of the PROGRAMMING
FUNCTIONAL SPECIFICATION and the PROJECT WORK PLAN, should
be thought of as a "feasibility study period."

- Reports to be produced.

The definition of completion should be explicit and detailed enough so that it is recognizable by those enacting the work.

3. The activity to be performed.

It is assumed that the activity to be performed between the START-POINT and END-POINT will include the following five broad classes of subactivities.

- Flowcharting and design.

- Computer coding.

- Computer program checkout.

- Documentation.

- Administrative and clerical work.

These activities will take place from the start of the DESIGN PHASE and will continue down to but not include MAINTENANCE by the external group.

The ACTIVITY TO BE PERFORMED may involve various numbers of personnel as well as various resources within a company. Also, it will entail varying amounts of the subactivities indicated above. It is important to note, however, that we will not call an effort a computer programming project unless it entails our definition of a START-POINT, END-POINT, and the ACTIVITY TO BE PERFORMED as given above.

4. An example.

One of the most catastrophic mistakes which a computer programming manager can make in estimating (ANALYSIS to MAINTENANCE) is to assume the existence of a project upon receipt of the EXTERNAL FUNCTIONAL SPECIFICATIONS--i.e., hypothesize the existence of a START-POINT, an END-POINT, and an ACTIVITY TO BE PERFORMED. Performance of the ANALYSIS PHASE must occur before any accurate estimating can begin to be achieved (except, of course, for well-known products; then the ANALYSIS PHASE isn't needed except to generate documentation).

It might be argued that if one had to wait for completion of a WORK PLAN and a PROGRAMMING FUNCTIONAL SPECIFICATION "in my company" in order to prepare estimates, no estimating would ever take place. This is commonly the case in, say, large business systems development efforts. However, completion of the plan and specifications does not mean they are complete.

What it does mean is that in such circumstances--i.e., where items are missing--the estimator must be careful to view the "total project" as being made up of parts; and he must base his estimates on these parts, giving assent to the fact that more may occur at a later time but not veering from the definition as applied to each part as he now knows it. This is best demonstrated by the hypothetical example given below:

An outside group comes to a programming manager and asks to have a management information system developed for the XYZ computer. The manager replies, "Fine, would you please give me an EXTERNAL FUNCTIONAL SPECIFICATION so that we may begin planning for what you would like done." The program manager for the outside group then says, "I can give you such an EXTERNAL FUNCTIONAL SPECIFICATION for some of the system; however, I am unable at this point in time to specify exactly what I want."

Upon receipt of the EXTERNAL FUNCTIONAL SPECIFICATION, the programming manager, aware that more will be added at a later time, should not make that which is not there his first object of concern. Rather, his primary concern must be with that which has been specified; he must ask himself the question, "Will this be enough to produce a meaningful WORK PLAN and PROGRAMMING FUNCTIONAL SPECIFICATION?" If the quality of the EXTERNAL FUNCTIONAL SPECIFICATION is such that no amount of analysis during the ANALYSIS PHASE can yield an adequate PROGRAMMING FUNCTIONAL SPECIFICATION and meaningful WORK PLAN, several courses of action are open to him.

- He can advise the outside group that the EXTERNAL FUNCTIONAL SPECIFICATION does not specify enough but that he will be pleased to perform a research activity.

- He can decline further work on the activity specified by the EXTERNAL FUNCTIONAL SPECIFICATION until agreement can be reached between his organization and the requesting authority as to what is wanted.

- If he assumes he has "enough," with the idea in mind that "more will be coming later," he then must be ready to enter the ANALYSIS PHASE--under the pressure of a gambler, at best.

Another great problem plaguing computer programming development groups is that external groups requesting projects think much differently from those performing them. The idea that the requesting group and the computer programming development group will perform some sort of a cooperative research and development effort is a dangerous presumption.

- The probability is that the requesting group is heavily concerned with the product and its time and cost without having too much regard for its means of development.

• The psychological orientation of the programming group is such that it usually will approach such a project as "something of interest" and hope that everyone will "understand." There is a great difference in viewpoint which must be recognized between the requesting agency and the programming department. The relationship is not unlike that which exists between the two parties to a contract in more general circumstances. Without some formal statement prior to project initiation there is bound to be an intergroup conflict.

C. PREPARING FOR TIME AND COST ESTIMATING

Assume that an EXTERNAL FUNCTIONAL SPECIFICATION has been provided. Assume that the ANALYSIS phase has been completed--that a project is defined. Thus the conditions for starting the project are known, the activities to be performed during the project are defined, and a definition of completion exists.* Developing the time and cost estimate for the project may now proceed from the WORK PLAN.

Sections II, III, and IV of the WORK PLAN (see Appendix 1) segment the project, describe staffing, and define support requirements. The estimator must now refine this information as indicated in the following sections.

D. FIXED COST FIXED TIME (FCFT) AND TIME AND MATERIAL (T&M) ESTIMATES

Computer programming estimates should take the form of either FCFT or T&M** as defined below:

• The fixed cost fixed time estimate.

A fixed cost fixed time estimate may be rendered when enough facts are known about the prospective project so that production uncertainties are reduced to the level of detailed judgments to be expected from the estimator with help from his staff. Nothing about the project is "unknown" (i.e., the estimator has confidence that everything can be produced).

---

*Do not confuse the conditions for completion with the means by which these conditions will be tested. Thus it may be known that a specific report in a specific format will be required; however, in performing the project one necessary part may be the design of a test to achieve the format.

**Bidding upon external work may require other forms; however, these are usually a variation of FCFT and T&M. Some people in the computer field differentiate those projects where an FCFT estimate can be made from those where a T&M estimate can be made by calling the former development projects and the latter research and development projects.

- The time and materials estimate.

    T&M estimates are to be given when vital pieces of information regarding the production of the product are missing yet it is known that a project <u>must take place</u>. Its START-POINT exists. An ACTIVITY TO BE PERFORMED and an END-POINT exist; however, these <u>will</u> be changed in time and hence are not to be considered fixed for the total project. In this case one may render a fixed cost fixed time <u>guess</u>, but not an estimate in the sense of this chapter. Only statements of incremental costs and upper-bound educated guesses can be made, but these will change.

After establishing the existence of a project, the estimator can decide whether or not it can be called FCFT or T&M by evaluating three major questions:

- What is the task?
- Who will perform the work?
- Is the logistical support available?

These questions have been answered in the "Work Plan Preparation" chapter. In addition, Charts 2 and 3 used to develop that plan should be available. Normally, they are included in an appendix to the plan as supporting material.

If any information is listed as "unknown" in the charts, the estimate can take only the T&M form.

E. <u>HOW TO PREPARE THE ESTIMATE</u>

The TIME AND COST ESTIMATE should be a short document patterned on the model which follows.

For an explanation of the use of the model see Appendix 1.

TIME AND COST ESTIMATE MODEL

TABLE OF CONTENTS

INTRODUCTION

Briefly state whatever background information seems relevant--project name, circumstances under which the effort was initiated, etc.

Explain whether the estimate is FCFT or T&M and why (reference ASSUMPTIONS, below).

Describe, generally, the content of the document and define how best to use it.

TIME

Indicate the expected duration of the project. Explain that this time figure has been used in the computation of the project cost.

Explain the logical process by which the projection was derived. This paragraph should reference a STAFFING PATTERN (Chart 3*), which should be included as an attachment to the document.

If the above staffing requirement can be met, the following schedule can be maintained:

Reproduce Section V of the WORK PLAN (TARGET DATES) here. The dates may be modified versions of those appearing in the first WORK PLAN, if the group leader's projections were proved inaccurate.

COST

State the estimated cost of the project and summarize how the figure was derived, referencing the STAFFING PATTERN--Chart 3--and Chart 4.

The cost of this project is estimated as follows:

(1) Personnel.

Name	Time	Monthly Salary	Salary Cost
Employee$_1$	T_1	S_1	$C_1 = S_1 \times T_1$
Employee$_2$	T_2	S_2	$C_2 = S_2 \times T_2$
.	.	.	.
.	.	.	.
.	.	.	.
.	.	.	.
Employee$_k$	T_k	S_k	$C_k = S_k \times T_k$
	COST	TOTAL	C

*All references to charts are to those given in the "Work Plan Preparation" chapter.

(2) Computer.

State the computer time requirement and the cost per hour for the operation of the equipment (reference, again, Chart 4). Finally, show the computation of the cost.

(3) Overhead.

Show the effect of the overhead multiplier, α, on the sum, C, derived in (1) above.

The corrected employee cost for this project is:

$$C' = \alpha \times C$$

(4) Unusual expenses.

List any unusual features of the project that will not be covered by the overhead multiplier, such as travel, excessive documentation requirements, etc. Each item should be described in detail and costed carefully. Finally, show the summation of the various items as follows:

	COST
Item$_1$	X_1
Item$_2$	X_2
.	.
.	.
.	.
Item$_k$	X_k
TOTAL	$\sum X_i = X$

(5) Computation.

$$\text{total cost} = C' + \text{computer cost} + X$$

ASSUMPTIONS

This section must be included. List the unknowns derived in Chart 1 and explain the assumptions that have been made regarding these items. Be very specific and clear.

CHECKLIST FOR
TIME AND COST ESTIMATING

	YES	NO
Has a WORK PLAN been prepared?	☐	☐
• Has the task been broken down into sufficiently small units in the WORK PLAN to lend credibility to the estimates contained therein?	☐	☐
• Are Charts 1 through 5* included as supporting material to the estimates?	☐	☐
• If not, is this material available elsewhere?	☐	☐
• Is it clear that there are no hidden assumptions in the WORK PLAN?	☐	☐
• Have historical files for past projects been used to support estimates?	☐	☐
Does the proposed project have a valid start-point definition?	☐	☐
Does the proposed project have a valid end-point definition?	☐	☐
Is the activity to be performed clearly defined?	☐	☐
Is the estimate to be fixed cost fixed time (FCFT)?	☐	☐
• Is the task definition fixed?	☐	☐
• Are all personnel to be involved known?	☐	☐
• Is the logistical support available?	☐	☐
• Are all items listed in Chart 1 known?	☐	☐

> IF ANY OF THE ABOVE FOUR QUESTIONS CANNOT BE ANSWERED AFFIRMATIVELY, THE ESTIMATE CANNOT BE FCFT.

	YES	NO
If some information is not available, is it possible to present an FCFT estimate on some subset of the work?	☐	☐

---

*All chart numbers in this checklist refer to those given in the "Work Plan Preparation" chapter.

NOTES

NOTES

IV. Specification Reviews

A. INTRODUCTION

Specification reviews are an important part of the project enactment activities; they provide a means of conformance control. Since they are made at critical points in the cycle, the reviews serve to delimit the stages of project evolution. Reviews mark points of transition from one stage of development to another.

1. General criteria.

The criteria for reviewing rest on three general bases: technical excellence, optimum resource utilization, and timely completion. Emphasis is not applied equally to these criteria at each of the review points. There is, for example, a time within the project cycle when resource utilization assumes greater weight than technical excellence because the latter has been assured.

2. Enactment flow.

The PROJECT ENACTMENT CHART in Chapter 1 depicts project development in a linear fashion, with review activities leading either to the next sequential function or, as the decision diamond implies, some other course of action based upon a management decision. Activities leading up to a given review, including the review itself, are frequently part of an iterative process. Each step may be repeated as often as required to assure conformance to the standards applicable at a given review point. For some parts of the cycle this repetition may be partial; one section of a project may require reworking at a given level while others proceed to a more advanced stage.

In general a project may be enacted in several roughly parallel sections. For, in addition to the necessity for modification at one stage which might require that some part of a project be reworked, there are interdependencies that require some sections to be carried out after others. Therefore, the enactment cycle as shown might be duplicated in parts many times for a complex system in order to assure smooth and satisfactory development.

3. Documents and reviews.

The documentation which serves as source material for the reviews always includes specifications in some form and, usually, a WORK PLAN.

As the project progresses and new information becomes available, these basic documents change character and new documentation is added. Specifications become increasingly detailed as the design develops; the WORK PLAN becomes more complete as some tasks are terminated and more accurate estimates can be made for others.

4. Personnel and reviews.

The major reviews are the ALPHA REVIEW, the BETA REVIEW, and the GAMMA REVIEW. These are conducted by the project engineer, the programming manager, the section supervisor, the staff supervisor, and the programming project leader. Members of the programming staff take part in WORK REVIEWS, USER DOCUMENTATION REVIEWS, and ERROR REPORT REVIEWS. In exceptional circumstances members of the programming group may be asked to give technical assistance in one or more of the other review meetings.

The project engineer and the programming project leader take part in all reviews. This means that, in addition to those reviews cited above, the programming project leader and the project engineer participate in MODIFICATION REVIEWS. The programming manager, the section supervisor, and the staff supervisor may be requested to provide specialized information at any of the review sessions.

B. THE ANALYSIS PHASE

The ALPHA REVIEW is the most critical from the point of view of project continuance. Documents considered are the PROGRAMMING FUNCTIONAL SPECIFICATIONS and the first version of the WORK PLAN. Both of these are based on the EXTERNAL FUNCTIONAL SPECIFICATIONS prepared by an outside agency.

Although work actually begins when the EXTERNAL FUNCTIONAL SPECIFICATIONS are given to the programming project leader, the effort prior to the ALPHA REVIEW is not considered to be part of the programming project. In fact, one objective of this review is to determine whether a project exists.*

1. Preparing for alpha review.

The programming project leader and the programming staff may be drawn from company personnel or from an outside group. In both cases the project leader and the programming staff perform the same functions.

The programming manager receives the EXTERNAL FUNCTIONAL SPECIFICATIONS and distributes copies to the section leader and the programming project leader. The latter gives copies to members of the programming group.

2. Specifications.

When programmers have received the EXTERNAL FUNCTIONAL SPECIFICATIONS, they write the first set of PROGRAMMING FUNCTIONAL

---

*A programming project is defined in detail in the "Time and Cost Estimating" chapter.

62

SPECIFICATIONS. In order to prepare these specifications, WORK REVIEWS may be held to clarify technical points.

The first PROGRAMMING FUNCTIONAL SPECIFICATIONS are quite elementary in form, being a simple restatement of project intents and aims in terms of the programming task envisioned to achieve them.

3.   Work plan.

At the same time, the programming project leader prepares his WORK PLAN. This WORK PLAN is a first estimate of the overall requirements and is refined as the project progresses. It is, however, extremely important in presenting the order of magnitude of the project.

4.   The alpha review.

The ALPHA REVIEW takes place when the PROGRAMMING FUNCTIONAL SPECIFICATIONS and the WORK PLAN are completed. These initial documents reveal the way in which the programming staff views the project system. Any large discrepancy between the intent of the design and its interpretation is made obvious by the time and resource estimates. At the same time any misconception of project magnitude on the part of the requesting agency is quickly rectified. It is here that a decision may be taken to do one of the following:

- Continue.
- Make a minor modification.
- Make a major modification.
- Suspend the effort.
- Abandon the effort.

5.   Review findings.

Should the ALPHA REVIEW bring to light a misunderstanding of the project specifications, the design cycle is repeated and a corrected WORK PLAN is prepared.

If the effort exceeds management planning in some area, steps may be taken early to secure the necessary resources.

In cases where a project lends itself to division into logical parts, one or more sections may be submitted for redesign or rescheduling while others go on to the DESIGN PHASE.

If the proposed project is judged not technically feasible or too expensive, it will not take place.

Information possibly affecting the implementation of the project system which becomes available at this review does not necessitate a new ANALYSIS cycle; it is incorporated, where required, into the next edition of the WORK PLAN. For example, if a COBOL processor which includes an assembly phase is under discussion, the programming manager might note that an existing PL/1 processor for the same machine includes an assembler.

Any possible savings of resources that might accrue from the use of existing programs within a current project is worked out in the WORK REVIEWS and reflected in a revised WORK PLAN.

6. Review report.

The CONFORMANCE REPORT comprises the findings of the review committee.

This report does not have a rigidly structured format; it should include, however:

- The WORK PLAN.

- A complete brief picture of the activity preceding its issuance.

- A collection of memos on the subject of the proposed project submitted by those members of the review committee who wish to comment.

A CONFORMANCE REPORT may be supplemented as a result of subsequent reviews held for sections of the project which were not fully approved at the initial meeting. The ALPHA REVIEW CONFORMANCE REPORT is a collection of material gathered in possibly more than one meeting; it cannot be regarded as complete until all parts of the project have entered the DESIGN PHASE.

Figure 1 is a flowchart for the ANALYSIS cycle. Activities are presented as they occur when the work is enacted. In those cases where outside groups participate, there may be a number of reviews, all treating submitted proposal material. There is then another decision path, which is that of selection of the group to carry out the project.

All activity descriptions given in this and subsequent sections outline activities in broad general terms. There can be great flexibility in the implementation to meet varying requirements of scope, staffing practice, etc. This material is intended as a guide to review activities and the manner in which they serve to control conformance to standards.

C. THE DESIGN PHASE

There are two formal DEVELOPMENT REVIEWS which take place in the DESIGN development stage of the enactment cycle. The first occurs periodically in DESIGN to insure that implementation is proceeding according to the agreed-upon specifications.

FIGURE 1   THE ANALYSIS PHASE

THE EXTERNAL FUNCTIONAL SPECIFICATIONS
are distributed.

The programming project leader and his staff meet to
discuss the EXTERNAL FUNCTIONAL SPECIFICATIONS.

The programming staff prepares the PROGRAMMING
FUNCTIONAL SPECIFICATIONS; the group leader prepares
a WORK PLAN.

The programming staff meets to review the PROGRAMMING
FUNCTIONAL SPECIFICATIONS.

Some parts of the specifications require reworking.

The PROGRAMMING FUNCTIONAL SPECIFICATIONS are
ready for review; the group leader checks the compatibility
of his estimates with the task defined.

If the WORK PLAN requires reworking, the group leader
makes necessary adjustments.

The ALPHA REVIEW COMMITTEE convenes.

The product has not been understood; it is ill-defined.

Resource and/or time estimates are unacceptable; a
reduced design is proposed; new EXTERNAL FUNCTIONAL
SPECIFICATIONS must be drawn up.

Resource estimates are unacceptable, and a reduced design
is unfeasible.

The PROGRAMMING FUNCTIONAL SPECIFICATIONS and the
WORK PLAN are approved as working documents; the DESIGN
stage begins.

CANCELLATION

The PROGRAMMING FUNCTIONAL SPECIFICATIONS as accepted after the ANALYSIS PHASE become the source material for the INTERNAL SYSTEMS SPECIFICATIONS (C), TEST SPECIFICATIONS, FLOWCHARTS (C), and the REFERENCE MANUALS.

When DESIGN begins, the programming staff may be greatly augmented. The programming personnel who reviewed the EXTERNAL FUNCTIONAL SPECI-FICATIONS and prepared the PROGRAMMING FUNCTIONAL SPECIFICATIONS usually represent only a part of the total staff required to conduct the project.

Programmers who write TEST SPECIFICATIONS, for example, are ordinarily taken from another group. TEST SPECIFICATIONS are ideally prepared by some outside agency--i.e., either a professional programming group or a special quality control and test section not responsible for producing a specific product.

1. Work reviews.

   WORK REVIEWS are held as specifications are prepared; TEST SPECI-FICATIONS are compared with the current INTERNAL SYSTEMS SPECI-FICATIONS and the REFERENCE MANUAL material to insure that the program action and use are clearly presented. WORK REVIEWS are attended by the programming project leader and his staff.

2. Reviewing user information.

   FLOWCHARTS and the INTERNAL SYSTEMS SPECIFICATIONS detail the manner in which the system is to be implemented. Both of these documents are highly technical in nature and are directed toward programming personnel.

   Their meaning in terms of the finished system is reflected in the REF-ERENCE MANUALS, which give a description of the finished product and its rules of use. The information provided about system action and the requirements for its use which is released at this time becomes source material for the final USER MANUAL.

   The USER MANUAL itself is written by a documentation team and is reviewed by members of the programming group for accuracy of content only. A parallel activity, proceeding during the DESIGN phase, is the preparation of user documentation. The writing of such documentation is properly the task of a professional documentation staff. Source material is supplied to the writer as soon as it is available for release.

   The decision to produce one or more preliminary user manuals is made on an individual basis, according to such considerations as project type, use, duration, and importance. In any case preliminary manuals that may be issued are termed preliminary because they lack some details-- not because they contain erroneous information.

The second group, using REFERENCE MANUALS, prepares test programs. The REFERENCE MANUALS should be sufficiently clear and complete to enable the programmers writing TEST SPECIFICATIONS to prepare test programs as soon as such specifications are approved. It may be impossible to write exhaustive tests at this time; more rigorous tests can be devised as details become firm.

Throughout development and implementation, meetings are held by the programmers, the group leader, the programming project leader, and the project engineer to study implementation methods and possibilities. Any minor modifications required as a result of this early analysis are incorporated into revised versions of the REFERENCE MANUALS.

3. Beta review.

An initial review is held when the programming staff has prepared the REFERENCE MANUALS, the TEST SPECIFICATIONS, the INTERNAL SYSTEMS SPECIFICATIONS (C), and any required revisions to the PROGRAMMING FUNCTIONAL SPECIFICATIONS.

The REFERENCE MANUALS are studied to detect any significant departure from standard practices for control usage, terminology employed, operating procedures, etc. If the REFERENCE MANUALS show that habitual procedures are not being applied, a minimal reanalysis may be required to provide a means of placing the product in a familiar environment for customer use.

*   PURPOSES AND CRITERIA.

    The BETA REVIEW is concerned with assuring continuity from the PROGRAMMING FUNCTIONAL SPECIFICATIONS to the INTERNAL SYSTEMS SPECIFICATIONS.

    Potential discrepancies between design and implementation become clear in the FLOWCHARTS (C) which are, at the end of the DESIGN PHASE, detailed coding directives. Members of the programming staff who have prepared the charts and specifications may be called upon to present the technical justification for some of the techniques chosen.

    In this review, comparison is made between the INTERNAL SYSTEMS SPECIFICATIONS (C) and the TEST SPECIFICATIONS to insure that system capabilities will be adequately exercised in the planned checkout.

    The test group evaluates the REFERENCE MANUALS as a programming tool for preparing jobs within the system during DESIGN. They are checked for clarity and comprehensibility as well as for completeness.

    Generally, the task of the BETA REVIEW is to insure that analysis proceeds according to the accepted specifications and that valid programming techniques are being employed. Should any of these checks reveal anomalies, the initial DESIGN PHASE is repeated in whole or in part until the fault is corrected.

- REVIEW RESULTS.

  Any major contradiction of the WORK PLAN, supported by technical documentation and WEEKLY PROGRESS REPORTS and revealed at this time, is noted by the programming project leader. This is the point at which additional resources may have to be requested to meet needs which have become apparent only after detailed analysis.

  When the last item of supporting documentation has been accepted:

    All technical details have been thoroughly investigated.

    The INTERNAL SYSTEMS SPECIFICATIONS (C) and the TEST SPECIFICATIONS describe the same system actions.

    FLOWCHARTS have been agreed upon as coding directives.

    REFERENCE MANUALS have been finalized.

- TECHNICAL DEVELOPMENT REPORT.

  The first DEVELOPMENT CONFORMANCE REPORT, like the DESIGN CONFORMANCE REPORT, provides information about project status and activity. It reflects any decisions made and their justifications.

4. Gamma review.

   The GAMMA REVIEW takes place almost immediately after the BETA REVIEW.

   This review considers the project status to date and predicts future progress. Any additional resource requests are made by way of a revised WORK PLAN.

   The purpose of this meeting is to present to management system capabilities and project resource utilization by the technical staff.

   While this review is being planned and carried out, the programming staff continues work. Changes to technical documents should not take place as a result of this review.

   The REFERENCE MANUALS describe the finished product that is to be delivered by the programming group. In this respect it is a form of contract. A REFERENCE MANUAL is not subject to significant change once it is issued.

● THE GAMMA REVIEW REPORT.

The CONFORMANCE REPORT issued at the end of the analysis/
development phase, like its predecessors, is a current status
report for the project. It contains more detailed technical information than the first two such reports and may simply expand
on them. There is far less likelihood that it will be incomplete
at the time it is issued, because it comes at a point of good
definition in product development and follows a period in which
experience in resource utilization has been gained.

D. DOCUMENTATION REVIEW

Figure 2, which follows, illustrates the order in which the various tasks are
accomplished during the DESIGN PHASE of project enactment. The role of
programming project leader may be taken by more than one individual; more
than one role, on the other hand, may be undertaken by the same individual.
Simplification or duplication of the activities described is a function of the
project being enacted.

Another activity parallels the DESIGN PHASE but is not shown in Figure 2
because there is no formal relationship of its activities to the other development tests--the production of user documents using the REFERENCE MANUALS
as source material.

Members of the technical staff make a content review of the proposed USER
MANUAL and OPERATIONS MANUAL. This review takes place after specifications are firm and the flowcharts are ready for use in coding.

The responsibility of the programming department with respect to documentation is that of insuring correctness and completeness of content. Questions of
style and presentation are the concern of technical writers.

After the technical review the documents are further edited for style only.
No significant changes in wording occur. (There may be cases in which information is necessarily lacking before coding.)

E. ACCEPTANCE EVALUATION

The DESIGN PHASE is followed by the implementation of the system and
product testing. Coding begins when the FLOWCHARTS (C) and the INTERNAL
SYSTEMS SPECIFICATIONS (C) are approved.

During the coding stage, modifications may be made to produce the INTERNAL
SYSTEMS SPECIFICATIONS (B) and FLOWCHARTS (B).

All personnel working on the project are kept informed of developments affecting their sphere of interest. Thus programmers writing test programs are
kept current about capabilities and conventions of use of the programs they
are testing; the technical writing department is given the latest available
descriptive information.

FIGURE 2   THE DESIGN PHASE

PROGRAMMING FUNCTIONAL SPECIFICATIONS are distributed to new staff members.

INTERNAL SYSTEMS SPECIFICATIONS (C), TEST SPECIFICA-TIONS, and REFERENCE MANUALS are developed; weekly progress reports are submitted.

The BETA REVIEW COMMITTEE convenes.

> A REFERENCE MANUAL requires modification.

> The INTERNAL SYSTEMS SPECIFICATIONS (C) require modification.

> The TEST SPECIFICATION is inadequate.

PROGRAMMING PROJECT LEADER prepares a revised WORK PLAN.

The GAMMA REVIEW COMMITTEE convenes.

> Resource estimates exceed expectation; some functions are deleted.

> Resource estimates exceed expectation, and no further paring down of the system is possible; CANCEL PROJECT.

> Project has deviated from that passed on in ALPHA REVIEW.

> Everything is satisfactory; continue.

1. Testing the product.

   Debugging takes place when coding is finished. Each programmer tests and corrects his own programs as they are completed.

   During the DEBUG PHASE each programmer is in a position to indicate, in his WEEKLY PROGRESS REPORTS, the particular areas of competence desirable for the person chosen to maintain his portion of the system.

   A general system test is carried out by the programming staff when all component programs have been checked out by their authors. Exhaustive system testing is then undertaken by the group which wrote the test programs. Every system capability is thoroughly tested and reports are made indicating the results. The original programming staff maintains the system during testing by the outside quality control agency.

2. Documenting for acceptance evaluation.

   System test staff members prepare test reports incorporating their procedures and findings--specifications, program listing, and all other pertinent reports.

   While system testing is in progress, the members of the original programming staff update their own documentation; the FLOWCHARTS (A), LISTING, and the INTERNAL SYSTEMS SPECIFICATIONS (A) are finalized during the SYSTEM TEST.

3. The acceptance review.

   At the completion of system testing by the test group an ACCEPTANCE REVIEW is held. Documents prepared by the programming staff and the test group serve as source material for a thorough investigation of system performance.

   When failure to meet standards is detected, additional modification and complete system retesting is required. Indications of failure to explore all system features may necessitate renewed system testing.

4. The acceptance report.

   The ACCEPTANCE CONFORMANCE REPORT is made up of test reports and review memos.

   There can be no partial release of the system into the next stage. The product system must be wholly acceptable for customer use at the end of the acceptance test stage.

F. ERROR REPORT REVIEWS

When approval is indicated, the system is released for customer use. Reports of suspected malfunction which are received during the initial period of use are reviewed by the programming project leader, the maintenance staff, and the programmers concerned. If a real system error is detected, a correction is made and distributed to users.

For those cases in which the suspected error is the result of misunderstanding of usage rules, a recommendation for clarification of the documentation may be made.

Throughout the early customer use a series of PRODUCT EVALUATION REPORTS are developed from the ERROR REVIEW sessions. These reports are the conformance documentation for this stage of enactment. When customer experience indicates that the system is trouble free, the maintenance period begins.

G. MODIFICATION REVIEWS

Requests for system modification may be sent by users from the earliest days of system release. Such requests are reviewed by the technical staff only as a means of evaluating the feasibility and acceptability of the proposed change. A report containing the technical evaluation is issued at the request of higher management.

CHECKLIST FOR

SPECIFICATION REVIEWS

THE ALPHA REVIEW IS AN EXAMINATION OF TWO
DOCUMENTS--THE PROGRAMMING FUNCTIONAL
SPECIFICATION AND THE WORK PLAN--TO SEE
WHETHER (1) THE TASK IS UNDERSTOOD AND (2)
RESOURCES ARE AVAILABLE TO PERFORM THE
PROPOSED PROJECT.

	YES	NO
Are PROGRAMMING FUNCTIONAL SPECIFICATIONS and the WORK PLAN distributed a week or more before the ALPHA REVIEW COMMITTEE convenes so that their content is known before discussion takes place?	☐	☐
Do all members of the committee have a copy of the EXTERNAL FUNCTIONAL SPECIFICATIONS?	☐	☐

Has the programming project leader invited for participation:

	YES	NO
• His section supervisor?	☐	☐
• The programming manager?	☐	☐
• Other interested parties within the programming department?	☐	☐
• The project engineer?	☐	☐
• Other interested personnel?	☐	☐
If there are problem areas in the PROGRAMMING FUNC-TIONAL SPECIFICATIONS, can some DESIGN WORK take place during re-ANALYSIS?	☐	☐
If project needs exceed available resources, can a substitute system be devised?	☐	☐

Does the CONFORMANCE REPORT include:

	YES	NO
• An overall view?	☐	☐
• The WORK PLAN?	☐	☐

- A collection of individual opinions submitted by committee members? ☐ ☐

> THE BETA REVIEW IS A TECHNICAL REVIEW; IT IS PRIMARILY CONCERNED WITH THE INTERNAL SYSTEMS SPECIFICATION (C) AND FLOWCHARTS (C).

Are the INTERNAL SYSTEMS SPECIFICATIONS (C), FLOWCHARTS (C), and REFERENCE MANUALS, etc. distributed a week or more before the BETA REVIEW COMMITTEE convenes so that their content can be known beforehand? ☐ ☐

Has the programming project leader invited to the meeting:

- His section supervisor? ☐ ☐

- The programming manager? ☐ ☐

- Other interested parties within the programming department? ☐ ☐

Are key staff members--group leaders--present to defend programming techniques if a detailed question arises? ☐ ☐

If re-DESIGN is necessary, can some CODING take place simultaneously? ☐ ☐

If re-DESIGN is necessary, do revisions of the PROJECT HISTORICAL RECORD reflect the additional effort? ☐ ☐

> THE GAMMA REVIEW IS ORIENTED TOWARD MANAGEMENT. THE REVISED WORK PLAN IS EXAMINED, AND IT IS DECIDED WHETHER RESOURCES ARE AVAILABLE FOR THE REMAINDER OF THE PROJECT. IN ADDITION CURRENT FUNCTIONAL DESCRIPTIONS ARE REVIEWED.

Are REFERENCE MANUALS and the revised WORK PLAN distributed a week or more before the BETA REVIEW COMMITTEE convenes so that their content is known beforehand? ☐ ☐

Has the programming project leader invited: YES   NO

- His section supervisor?   ☐   ☐

- The programming manager?   ☐   ☐

- Other interested parties within the programming   ☐   ☐
  department?

- The project engineer?   ☐   ☐

- Other interested company personnel?   ☐   ☐

If the WORK PLAN shows that the completion date will not be   ☐   ☐
met, is it possible to prepare some usable subset of the
system by that time?

If not, within the present design can some re-DESIGN make   ☐   ☐
this possible?

If resource estimates are higher than current availability,   ☐   ☐
can functions be cut to reduce cost?

Are high estimates due to an overly unusual approach on   ☐   ☐
the part of the implementers?

If so, can re-DESIGN reduce costs?   ☐   ☐

> THE ACCEPTANCE REVIEW IS HELD TO DETER-
> MINE WHETHER THE PRODUCT CAN BE RE-
> LEASED FOR CUSTOMER USE.

Has the SYSTEM TEST been of sufficient duration to simulate   ☐   ☐
actual field usage?

Do test programs conform to the previously approved TEST   ☐   ☐
SPECIFICATIONS?

Were all reported errors corrected, and was the test sequence   ☐   ☐
repeated from the start?

	YES	NO
Has a SYSTEM TEST log been kept?	☐	☐
Has an EVALUATION REPORT been prepared by the TESTING GROUP?	☐	☐
Have these documents been circulated and read by the members of the ACCEPTANCE REVIEW COMMITTEE?	☐	☐

THE DOCUMENTATION REVIEW IS THE REVIEW OF VARIOUS USER MANUALS BY THE IMPLEMENTERS TO INSURE THAT ALL INFORMATION TO BE ISSUED TO THE FIELD IS CORRECT.

	YES	NO
Has the programming staff subjected source documents for technical writers (REFERENCE MANUALS) to a thorough examination?	☐	☐
● Have the technical writers had difficulty understanding REFERENCE material?	☐	☐
● Has the TESTING GROUP shown an understanding of the system after reading the REFERENCE MANUALS?	☐	☐
● Have improved versions of the REFERENCE MANUALS been issued to cover areas where misunderstanding has been noted?	☐	☐
Do the PROGRAMMER REFERENCE portions of the USER MANUALS represent the system accurately?	☐	☐
Do the OPERATIONS REFERENCE portions of the USER MANUALS represent the system accurately?	☐	☐
Have early versions of the USER MANUALS been used by the TESTING GROUP for test preparation?	☐	☐
Did SYSTEM TESTING simulate customer use through instructions to personnel to use OPERATOR'S MANUALS before their issuance to the field?	☐	☐

NOTES

V. Project Enactment Checkpoints

A. INTRODUCTION

This chapter presents a discussion of the meaning and concepts involved in establishing PROJECT ENACTMENT CHECKPOINTS. Basically, two primary checkpoint types are defined below: SUBPRODUCT CHECKPOINTS and ACTIVITY CHECKPOINTS.

The idea of establishing PROJECT ENACTMENT CHECKPOINTS is very important to the proper management of a project. It allows a common understanding of what is meant when reporting takes place through a common "communications language" geared to a specific project. The next two sections discuss the two primary checkpoint types. It should be clear that other types can be established.

B. SUBPRODUCT CHECKPOINTS

A PROJECT ENACTMENT CHECKPOINT may be defined as a date at which some physical evidence of progress is expected to appear. Checkpoints provide a frame of reference for the progress reporting system, which divides the overall effort into a series of subtasks each of which can be associated with a visible subproduct.

Included in the PROJECT WORK PLAN is a section entitled TARGET DATES, which defines the expected work schedule. The schedule consists of PROJECT ENACTMENT CHECKPOINTS and the dates at which work upon subproducts is expected to begin and end.

The use of PROJECT ENACTMENT CHECKPOINTS, as defined above, is to evaluate progress reports and maintain the PERT CHARTS. Progress reports are arranged by columns, each referring to a subtask. By comparing weekly reports with the relevant TARGET DATES stated as a project week number, a clear picture of progress to date can be formed.

In order to evaluate subproducts when they appear, their precise definitions are necessary. Some subproducts which can define PROJECT ENACTMENT CHECKPOINTS are sketched in the supplement to this chapter. It should be clear that the types of subproduct PROJECT ENACTMENT CHECKPOINTS to be established are highly dependent upon the scope and type of project being enacted. All of the documents shown on the PROJECT ENACTMENT CHART in the Introduction--Chapter 1--can be considered PROJECT ENACTMENT CHECKPOINTS.

The chapters on WORK PLAN PREPARATION and TIME AND COST ESTIMATING will be of value to the PROGRAMMING PROJECT LEADER when he derives his subproduct PROJECT ENACTMENT CHECKPOINTS. In addition the following rules should be kept in mind:

- The dates at which reviews will be held should be determined after project checkpoints have been established--not before.

- Checkpoints must be established at the component level as well as at the project level.

- Checkpoints at the project level and at the component level should differ. An INTERNAL SYSTEMS SPECIFICATION for the project is a collection of component INTERNAL SYSTEMS SPECIFICATIONS plus an overview document. Time must be allowed for the assembly and editing of the project-level specifications.

- A document specifying checkpoints at the component level should be distributed to the project staff at the start of the DESIGN PHASE. The WEEKLY REPORT form (shown in Chapter VI) is convenient for this purpose. The tenth box of each column is to be filled in with the desired completion date for the subproduct in question.

C. ACTIVITY CHECKPOINTS

A PROJECT ENACTMENT CHECKPOINT may be defined as the completion of the performance of an activity--DESIGN, BETA REVIEW, etc.

The PROJECT ENACTMENT CHART suggests the following activity checkpoints:

1. ANALYSIS.
2. ALPHA REVIEW.
3. DESIGN.
4. BETA REVIEW.
5. GAMMA REVIEW.
6. CODE.
7. DEBUG.
8. SYSTEM TEST.
9. ACCEPTANCE REVIEW.
10. CUSTOMER ACCEPTANCE.

It should be clear that these checkpoints may exist per module, per set of modules, and for the entire project. Whatever the case, completion of the given activities will establish the meeting of checkpoints.

D. EVALUATION OF PROJECT STATUS

PERT NETWORKS for projects enacted in other fields are often updated using only "time spent" in various tasks. This method is effective where progress is not highly people dependent.

PERT can only measure the best guesses of management. These guesses can be improved greatly by noting actual performance. By defining the project as the completion of a series of well-defined subproducts or activities--CHECK-POINTS--PERT can be used to better advantage.

Checkpoints are also valuable in determining the uniformity of the effort; the following example is included to point this out.

EXAMPLE

The shorthand notation of Chapter VI--"Progress Reporting"--is employed in the PROJECT WEEKLY REPORT chart which follows. Since no explanation of this notation appears in this chapter, it is suggested that the reader refer to the reporting chapter before continuing. This report, submitted at the end of project week 5, should be interpreted as follows:

Assume that the following checkpoints have been established: The PROGRAM-MER'S MANUAL is due by PROJECT WEEK 10, as are the INTERNAL SYS-TEMS SPECIFICATION (C) and the FLOWCHARTS (C). But after five weeks the PROGRAMMER'S MANUAL is only 20 percent complete and the INTERNAL SYSTEMS SPECIFICATION (C) is only 30 percent finished. The 80 percent figure given for FLOWCHARTS (C) is encouraging but does not necessarily imply that the project is now on schedule.

By averaging the three completion figures, it might be argued that work for this phase is about 43 percent finished in half the allotted time period--not significantly behind schedule.

Experience has shown, however, that the most efficient way to enact a programming project is to keep project documents progressing at the same rate as the coding/flowcharting effort. The wide discrepancy between progress figures--20 percent to 80 percent completion--indicates that the effort may be far behind schedule.

A 20 percent lag in any column of the PROJECT WEEKLY REPORT is significant enough to warrant an explanatory comment in the report.

PROJECT WEEKLY REPORT

FUNCTIONAL SPEC	PRO-GRAMMER'S MANUAL	INTERNAL SYSTEMS SPEC (C)	FLOWCHARTS (C)	CODING	CHECKOUT	SYSTEM INTEGRATION
3	5	5	5			

CHECKLIST FOR

PROJECT ENACTMENT CHECKPOINTS

	YES	NO
Have checkpoints been established in the WORK PLAN?	☐	☐
Is there a well-defined subprogram or activity associated with each checkpoint?	☐	☐
Have checkpoints been noted on a large chart which appears in the programming area?	☐	☐
Is the progress-reporting system tied to the concept of checkpoints?	☐	☐
Are PERT DIAGRAMS updated, using a percentage completed toward the production of a physical product rather than just time spent?	☐	☐
Have the dates for scheduled review sessions been determined after checkpoints were derived--not before?	☐	☐
Are checkpoints established at the component level as well as at the project level?	☐	☐

SUPPLEMENT TO PROJECT ENACTMENT CHECKPOINTS

The following are examples of subproduct definitions for PROJECT ENACT-
MENT CHECKPOINTS. The proper place for specifying all such checkpoints
is in the PROJECT WORK PLAN. Usually, the detailed specification of document checkpoints is a section of the plan entitled "Documentation Plan."

1. Reference manuals.

    REFERENCE MANUALS should be produced in pairs--one manual for
    operations use and the other for programming use. For example, assume
    that REFERENCE MANUALS for an operating system are to be produced.

    The OPERATOR'S REFERENCE should have at minimum the following
    headings:

    - INTRODUCTION
    - SYSTEM DESCRIPTION
    - CONTROL RECORDS
    - SYSTEM OPERATION
        SET-UP PROCEDURE
        ORGANIZATION OF JOBS FOR PROCESSING
        LOADING PROCESS
        RUNNING THE SYSTEM
        OPERATOR INTERRUPT PROCEDURE
        RESTART PROCEDURE
        OPERATOR MESSAGES AND APPROPRIATE RESPONSES
    - OPERATOR ACCOUNTING PROCEDURE

    The PROGRAMMER'S REFERENCE must cover these topics:

    - INTRODUCTION
    - STANDARDS AND CONVENTIONS USED IN THE MANUAL
    - HARDWARE ENVIRONMENT
    - SOFTWARE ENVIRONMENT
    - PROGRAMMER'S INTERFACE WITH THE SYSTEM
        SYSTEM REQUIREMENTS
        PROGRAMMING CONSIDERATIONS
    - USAGE
        PROGRAM IDENTIFICATIONS
        PROCESSING OPTIONS
        DEBUGGING AIDS
        · · ·
        · · ·
        SEGMENTATION
    - JOB ORGANIZATION
    - INPUT-OUTPUT FACILITIES
    - STORAGE REQUIREMENTS

2. Internal systems specifications.

The INTERNAL SYSTEMS SPECIFICATION for a large system consists of two elements:

- An OVERVIEW document.
- A collection of component specifications.

A SYSTEM OVERVIEW includes:

- INTRODUCTION
    DESIGN PHILOSOPHY
    SOFTWARE ENVIRONMENT
    HARDWARE ENVIRONMENT
    STANDARDS AND CONVENTIONS USED IN THE MANUAL
- COMPONENT DIRECTORY
- SYSTEM LAYOUT
- STORAGE LAYOUT
- OVERALL FLOWCHARTS
- GLOBAL IDENTIFIERS (TABLE NAMES AND LAYOUT, etc.)
- DATA DESCRIPTION
    TAPE

    . . .

    . . .
    DISC
- GLOSSARY OF SYSTEM TERMINOLOGY

A complete COMPONENT SPECIFICATION should be patterned as follows:

- PURPOSE
- RELATION TO SYSTEM
- ENTRY CONDITIONS
- EXIT CONDITIONS
- GLOBAL REFERENCES
- STORAGE REQUIREMENTS
- NARRATIVE FLOWCHARTS (multilevel)

INTERNAL SYSTEMS MANUALS evolve throughout the life of the project. At various points during enactment a certain level of completeness is expected. The degree of completeness is indicated by level indicators--C, B, and A. The meaning of the level indicators is discussed below.

- INTERNAL SYSTEMS SPECIFICATION (C): This is the first version of the specification appearing at the close of the ANALYSIS phase. It contains every paragraph heading that will appear in the eventual A-level document. Content, however, is not as complete. This document is sufficiently detailed to act as a basis for coding. During the CODING phase detail not known a priori will be filled in.

- INTERNAL SYSTEMS SPECIFICATION (B): An expanded version of the C-level document. To all appearances this is the final document, reflecting the coding intricacies of the program. It may, however, contain errors, owing to the fact that this detailed specification appears before the DEBUG phase begins.

- INTERNAL SYSTEMS SPECIFICATION (A): Although the Class B document is complete, it may contain errors. The reason for B- and A-level distinctions is that extensive revision almost always occurs between the start of the DEBUG phase and the end of the SYSTEM TEST, which must be reflected in technical documentation.

3. Flowcharts.

FLOWCHARTS are included in the INTERNAL SYSTEMS SPECIFICATION and reflect the same degree of completeness as their parent document.

4. Listings.

The first LISTING is the project subproduct, which indicates that CODING is complete. This and subsequent listings should reflect the principles of documentation advanced in the CODING chapter.

NOTES

NOTES

VI. Progress Reporting

A. INTRODUCTION

This chapter contains a description of a computer programming project status reporting system. It is called REPSYS.*

The primary objectives of REPSYS are:

- To facilitate the collection and display of data regarding the status of work on a program or system of programs in development.

- To minimize the amount of verbal communication and personnel interaction required in obtaining project status data.

- To provide a common concept of project status throughout all levels of programming personnel and their management and others.

The above objectives of REPSYS are to be achieved in its design, development, and installation. These objectives, while an end in themselves, are secondary to the reasons for the existence of REPSYS. They are all directed toward aiding management in discharging certain duties. These may be (basically) categorized under the following four headings:

- Scheduling and control--assignment of schedules and establishment of procedures for periodically checking on adherence to them.

- Allocation of resources--assignment of personnel, machine time, and other resources.

- Project strategy--planning for optimal task execution.

- Evaluation of performance--comparison of finished operation with original conception; highlighting those factors responsible for satisfactory or unsatisfactory aspects of the operation.

In order for REPSYS to fulfill its charter and for management to succeed in properly discharging its duties as given above, the following must (minimally) occur:

- REPSYS must be designed, developed, and installed properly.

- Management must know (or learn) how to discharge its duties properly.

- The entire staff at all levels must cooperate fully.

The contents of this chapter are dedicated to the fulfillment of the proper design, development, and installation of REPSYS. Management and staff must find a means of insuring the fulfillment of the last two items above.

---

*Stands for REPorting SYStem.

B.   REPSYS--OVERVIEW

There are three sections to REPSYS.

1.   The personnel reporting procedure.

This section defines procedures by which personnel at various levels will be required to report their activities.

It is assumed that no project has more than two levels of management and that no manager has more than ten personnel reporting to him. (The lesser the number, the greater the accuracy in reporting.)*

2.   The project status display procedure.

This procedure defines a method by which project status and other relevant information may be displayed.

The project status display information is derived from the PERSONNEL REPORTING PROCEDURE, described in Section C, below.

3.   The summarization and evaluation procedure.

This procedure defines a means by which management personnel may summarize data acquired through the PERSONNEL REPORTING PROCEDURE intended to be displayed under the PROJECT STATUS DISPLAY PROCEDURE. Also, methods of compiling historical information will be presented.

4.   Discussion.

REPSYS is a project-oriented reporting system. The following concepts underlie its principles of operation.

● At any time during the normal work week the programming organization has a real and a virtual** organizational structure.

---

*The implications of this assumption are that no project will have more than 111 people--an absolute maximum in controllable size--and reports are summarized at maximum twice. The staffing parameter should be viewed as theoretically possible to be achieved but definitely not recommended. Recent industrywide development fiascoes in software and applications are substantiation for this comment.

**"Virtual" being in essence or effect but not in fact. Thus it is recognized that project management may not have recognition as bona fide management in the hierarchical structure of the department (and perhaps justifiably).

- The virtual organization may either coincide with the real organization or not coincide with the real organization; but it always defines the structure through which reporting takes place most accurately.

- REPSYS is intended to operate within the virtual organization. From here on, all references to organization, departmental organization, etc. are to the virtual organization unless otherwise noted.

- It is important that all programming personnel always consider themselves part of at least one project within the organization.

- If a staff member is part of more than one project, the projects with which his efforts are associated should be of increasing size and ordered by inclusion; otherwise, he is a manager. For example, consider the following departmental organization chart.

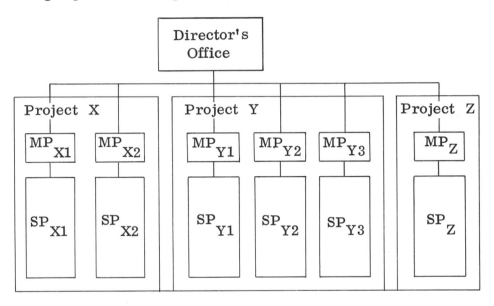

NOTE:

MP_{Xi} means Manager of Project Xi where i=1 or 2.

MP_{Yi} means Manager of Project Yi where i=1 or 2.

MP_Z means Manager of Project Z.

Similar interpretations for S, meaning Staff, are clear for SP_{Xi}, SP_{Yi}, and SP_Z.

(a) Note that P_{X1} and P_{X2} are included in Project X; P_{Y1}, P_{Y2}, and P_{Y3} are included in Project Y; and Project Z has but one component subproject.

(b) A member of the staff SP_{X1} is also a member of Project X. Thus he may be thought of as being on two projects. Indeed, he may actually work on two--e.g., he may have primary responsibility in coordination of P_{X1} output with P_{X2} output. However, this is different from, say, working <u>within</u> the P_{X1} group <u>and</u> the P_{X2} group. This leads to the next and important principle, under Item (C), below.

(c) The director's office is expected to manage the MP_{Xi}, MP_{Yi}, and MP_Z.

- No staff member can have responsibilities upon two equivalent-level projects. This principle, while easy to understand, is frequently violated with unhappy results.

Two "equivalent level" projects need not necessarily be in equivalent areas. Thus requiring a programmer to work on a program module and at the same time to engage in sales is a mistake. While similar situations may exist in other fields with satisfactory results achieved, programming does not allow it.

Preparing a computer program or system of programs within a given time frame for a given cost requires the full attention of the programming staff. Idle time during project enactment most frequently indicates either poor programming practices or poor management.

Given the above principles, REPSYS is intended to function according to the following rules:

R1. Each member of the programming development staff will submit a weekly report (no matter what he is doing).

R2. Each project manager will summarize the information obtained from the staff members reporting to him and prepare his report for the director's office. This report will be completed weekly also.

R3. If a project has more than one manager--i.e., is composed of subprojects--the director's office will be responsible for summarizing the reports of the managers. Note that no more than two official levels of summarization can take place.

R4. Project status information will be posted weekly on control boards.

R5. The director's office will compile a project historical record.

R6. The director's office will be responsible for informing higher management of project status, informing project management of its requirements, and analyzing report data to recommend alternative work strategies in times of unforeseen change, unexpected success, and/or trouble.

R7. If management requires a monthly report, the project manager will prepare it as per the model report given in this section.

C.   THE PERSONNEL REPORTING PROCEDURE

1.   The weekly report.

This report, to be prepared by each programmer, consists primarily of a chart indicating progress to date and anticipated progress for the next week. Since one or more system components may be assigned to a single programmer, the chart allows multiple JOB* name entries. Also, since each JOB involves an identifiable set of activities, the chart is broken down into the following categories:

- PROGRAMMER'S FUNCTIONAL SPECIFICATION.

- REFERENCE MANUAL.

- INTERNAL SYSTEMS SPECIFICATION (C).

- INTERNAL SYSTEMS SPECIFICATION (B).

- INTERNAL SYSTEMS SPECIFICATION (A).

- FLOWCHARTS (C).

- FLOWCHARTS (B).

- FLOWCHARTS (A).

- CODING.

- CHECKOUT.

- SYSTEM INTEGRATION.

THE PROJECT ENACTMENT CHART given in Chapter I, "Introduction," contains an enactment procedure which has certain checkpoints.   These linearly describe the series of events through which a project must go as it proceeds toward completion.   These events presuppose the existence of certain items, most of which are documentation of one kind or another.

Note that the letters C, B, and A are associated with both INTERNAL SYSTEMS SPECIFICATIONS and FLOWCHARTS.   These evolve from a first version (level C) to a final version (level A) during the life of the project.   Thus at certain stages in project enactment these documents must have attained a certain level of completeness.

Referring to the PROJECT ENACTMENT CHART, class C relates to DESIGN, class B to CODING, and class A to the DEBUG and SYSTEM TEST phases. It follows that, for example, the DESIGN PHASE of the project

---

*JOB refers to a programming assignment; it should not be interpreted in the "batch processing" sense of the word.

cannot be considered complete until all WEEKLY REPORTS indicate 100 percent completion of class $\underline{C}$ flowcharts and specifications.

The WEEKLY REPORT is a chart with a two-dimensional breakdown.

Each box, defined horizontally by an activity subdivision and vertically by a job or component name,* is further broken down into ten units. If an activity is 30 percent complete, this is indicated by a proper entry in the third square from the left in that box.

Progress to date and anticipated progress for the next week is indicated by placing appropriate PROJECT WEEK NUMBERS** in the array of boxes.

The scheme is best illustrated by an example. For a certain JOB, say JOB_1, assume the following report is received at the end of PROJECT WEEK 3.

ACTIVITY / JOB	FUNCTIONAL SPECIFICATION	REFERENCE MANUAL	INTERNAL SYSTEMS SPEC ( )	FLOWCHARTS
JOB $_1$	3		3 / 4	3 4

The portion of this report shown indicates that:

(a) The FUNCTIONAL SPECIFICATION was completed during PROJECT WEEK 3.

(b) Work has not yet begun on the REFERENCE MANUALS.

(c) Some work was done on the INTERNAL SYSTEMS SPECIFICATION prior to PROJECT WEEK 3, but no progress in this area is expected during the next week.

(d) Approximately 20 percent of the flowcharting is complete, and it is expected that by the end of next week 50 percent will be finished.

A list of representative reporting situations appears below. For simplicity of presentation JOB names and ACTIVITY designators are ignored and a single box is shown with its interpretation to the right. Again, PROJECT WEEK 3 is assumed.

---

*Each system under development should be broken down into component parts, each associated with some logical function. When programming tasks are assigned, it may be advantageous, under the proper circumstances, to segment the work further. If this occurs, the word "component" no longer is applicable. JOB is a more general term meaning programming assignment.

**This life of the project is broken down into PROJECT WEEKS numbered from 1 to $\underline{n}$.

The task has been completed.

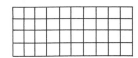

30 percent completed to date.
60 percent will be finished by next week.

No progress to date.

The task was completed on a
week prior to the current
reporting week.

80 percent finished today but no
anticipated progress next week.

50 percent completion was reported
last time. Something has happened
to cause this week's completion
estimate to be less (30 percent).
As of next week 60 percent of
the work will be finished.

The last possibility in the list, being exceptional, may require an explanatory note. Space is provided in the form for REMARKS.

Note that the number of <u>rows per job</u>--four--given on the WEEKLY REPORT form is to allow for flexibility in reporting various conditions. For example, if the programmer wished to report "no progress anticipated" between weeks 3 and 4, he could not do it without more than one row.

<u>Every report should contain at minimum three numbers per ACTIVITY</u> (except the first and last report on that ACTIVITY). These should represent:

    What was accomplished last week.
    The current status of the ACTIVITY.
    What is expected to be accomplished next week.

A sample report is given in Section F, "Sample Reports."

2.   <u>The project weekly report.</u>

The project leader is responsible for preparation of the PROJECT WEEKLY REPORT. Its preparation is very similar to that of the WEEKLY REPORT, except that the techniques described in Section E, "Summarization and Evaluation Procedure," must be employed.

A sample report is given in Section F.

3.   The project monthly report.

A monthly report, which is more explanatory than the weekly reports, may be required on certain projects. Section F, below, contains a sample monthly report. Note that this sample is in two parts: a table of contents and a second section explaining the items listed in the table of contents. The model report is not intended to restrict the project leader specifically and solely to its structure and content. It is included here to suggest a minimal subject-matter content from which the report writer may want to proceed.

D.   THE PROJECT STATUS DISPLAY PROCEDURE

Each week the director's office will receive PROJECT WEEKLY REPORTS. These, summarizing the information gathered from the project staff, will represent information to be posted on the PROJECT STATUS CONTROL BOARD (see Section G, "Sample Displays") following proper analysis (see Section E, "Summarization and Evaluation Procedure").

The PROJECT STATUS CONTROL BOARD should be professionally constructed as per the diagram given in CHART 1. Adhesive or, preferably, magnetized number plates to represent project week numbers (for use as described in Section C, "Personnel Reporting Procedure") will be posted on the board. The imaginative use of color-coded number plates may be employed to represent various conditions such as early, late, suspended, etc.

The procedure will be as follows:

1.   PROJECT WEEKLY REPORTS will be submitted no later than 12 noon on the first work day of each week.

2.   The director's office will check off receipt of the report on a master projects check list.

3.   Reports will be reviewed* and the PROJECT STATUS CONTROL BOARD UPDATED.

It may be of value to organize the projects on the PROJECT STATUS CONTROL BOARD into logical groups for ease of cross reference, etc.

Other displays are discussed in Section G, "Sample Displays."

---

*Whether or not review can take place, the update should.

E. THE SUMMARIZATION AND EVALUATION PROCEDURE

1. General.

Programming development within an organization is usually subdivided into projects. Each project is further subdivided into its logical components. A component might consist of more than one programming assignment or JOB.

All progress evaluation is based on information derived from the WEEKLY REPORT. It is theoretically possible, within the reporting structure described in REPSYS, to develop higher-level reports directly from reports made at the JOB or COMPONENT level.

● EXAMPLE:

Suppose a system consists of ten components each of which represents one-tenth of the implementation effort, and suppose that the work is to be enacted by ten equally competent programmers.

To derive a PROJECT WEEKLY REPORT (see Section F, "Sample Reports"), sum percentages on the WEEKLY REPORTS on the project by ACTIVITY. Then the "percentage completed" figure per ACTIVITY can be derived by dividing by ten.

Generally speaking, the ith JOB of a system having n JOBS represents some fraction, a_i, of the required effort. An expression for the "percentage completed" figure of an ACTIVITY can be formalized as the average:

$$\frac{1}{n} \sum_{i=1}^{n} a_i p_i$$

where p_i represents the percentage progress for JOB_i per ACTIVITY. This averaging method could readily be extended for use in the preparation of successively higher-level reports.

Other theoretical "games" can be played with WEEKLY REPORTS on a project. For example, one might attempt to construct a coefficient of overall completeness from a specific report by using an averaging method similar to that above by assigning a set of weights $(k_1, k_2, \ldots k_{10})$ to the various ACTIVITIES. Summing percentage-completion figures horizontally across the page the average:

$$\frac{1}{n} \sum_{i=1}^{n} a_i k_i$$

can be formed. Abstractly, this figure represents the state of completion of the work summarized in the chart.

- IMPORTANT REMARKS.

  Such methods must be applied with extreme caution. This system of reporting is only a convenient way of representing observations. The value of the scheme lies in its pictorial quality; a complete summary can easily be confined to a page and can be appreciated at a glance. An algebraic treatment is possible only if the figures involved are concrete quantities. The percentages given in a report are at best approximations.

  It is also important to consider the many questionable assumptions that must be made in formalizing the procedure:

  - Programmers are all assumed to be of equal ability.

  - The effort necessary for the implementation of a system is assumed to be expressible as the sum of the efforts required for each component part. (This ignores completely the problem of system module interrelationships.)

  - It is assumed that the cumulative error produced by summing approximations will not alter the accuracy of the result.

  Other false assumptions might be pointed out, but a lengthy discussion of this topic is not in order here. The point is that care must be taken in the interpretation of WEEKLY REPORTS so that MONTHLY and WEEKLY PROJECT REPORTS will provide as accurate a picture of events as possible.

Notwithstanding the above remarks, experience with use of the procedure suggested here very quickly allows the project leader the luxury of placing reasonable bounds upon project status per ACTIVITY and for the project itself. Also, the weekly conclusions derived plus the experience of deriving them has been seen to be highly instrumental in "homing in" on early and accurate project status reporting.

Other summations than those given above suggest themselves. The REPSYS user, once comfortable with its procedures, will find this summation technique, while far from perfect, a simple, meaningful, and sufficiently accurate tool.

- Procedure to produce the PROJECT WEEKLY REPORT:

  (1) Scan each report noting all instances of unusually strong or unusually disappointing progress.*

  (2) Compare each with the PROJECT HISTORICAL RECORD (see Item 2, below) and note all unexplained discrepancies.

---

*The project leader should discuss all exceptional reports with their author(s) in order to develop a stronger sense of the reality of the situation.

(3) Using the project implementation network, determine whether anticipated progress is realistic.

(4) Follow the summation procedure given at the beginning of this section for each project.

(5) Fill out the PROJECT WEEKLY REPORT.

(6) Fill in this week's entry in the PROJECT HISTORICAL RECORD.

2. The project historical record.

It is the responsibility of the project leader to merge several WEEKLY REPORTS into a meaningful evaluation of the overall project standing. This is called preparing the PROJECT WEEKLY REPORT. From these the PROJECT HISTORICAL RECORD, which summarizes data over the entire implementation period, is prepared.

The PROJECT HISTORICAL RECORD is included in the MONTHLY PROJECT REPORT. In addition, it, along with other related administrative documents, is retained for future reference after the completion of work.

The PROJECT HISTORICAL RECORD is a chart similar to the PROJECT WEEKLY REPORT. Both use the same convention: a project week number written in a square indicates the work completed that week in some particular area. The primary differences between the two are as follows:

● The PROJECT HISTORICAL RECORD has more columns. A separate column is provided for specifications and flowcharts in classes A, B, and C.

● All past weeks' entries are retained.

For example, consider the following chart entry and its interpretation.

This means 10 percent completion by the end of Week 1, 20 percent after Week 2, 30 percent after Week 3, no progress during Weeks 4 and 5, 50 percent completion by the end of Week 6, and so forth.

A sample PROJECT HISTORICAL RECORD is given in Section F, "Sample Reports."

Notice that no space for "Remarks" is provided. Remarks for all unusual events represented in the chart can be found by referring to the appropriate WEEKLY REPORT. The PROJECT HISTORICAL RECORD in this way acts as a cross-reference document for all reports.

F. <u>SAMPLE REPORTS</u>

FORMATS FOR:

        WEEKLY REPORT
        PROJECT WEEKLY REPORT
        PROJECT HISTORICAL RECORD
        PROJECT MONTHLY REPORT

CHART 1

WEEKLY REPORT

NAME _____

DATE _____

ACTIVITY / JOB	FUNCTIONAL SPEC	REFERENCE MANUAL	INTERNAL SYSTEM SPEC ( )	FLOWCHARTS ( )	CODING	CHECKOUT	SYSTEM INTEGRATION
JOB_1							
JOB_2							
JOB_3							
JOB_4							

REMARKS: This section may be left blank. The blank parentheses in columns 3 and 4 must be filled in with the appropriate level number. All unusual circumstances reported in the chart deserve comment. If more room is needed, attach additional pages to the report.

CHART 2

PROJECT WEEKLY REPORT

PROJECT NAME _____
MANAGER _____
DATE _____

FUNCTIONAL SPEC	REFERENCE MANUAL	INTERNAL SYSTEM SPEC( )	FLOWCHARTS ( )	CODING	CHECKOUT	SYSTEM INTEGRATION

REMARKS: This may be left blank. Discuss any unusual developments affecting reported or anticipated progress. If a particular component is at fault or for some other reason deserves a special comment, attach the relevant WEEKLY REPORT to this form. Also, do not hesitate to include additional pages if this space is inadequate.

CHART 3
PROJECT HISTORICAL RECORD

PROJECT NAME _____
STARTING DATE _____

JOB₁

NAME	FUNCTIONAL SPECIFICATION	REFERENCE MANUAL	CODING	CHECKOUT	SYSTEM INTEGRATION

	INTERNAL SYSTEM SPEC		FLOWCHARTS		
C	B	A	C	B	A

JOB₂

NAME	FUNCTIONAL SPECIFICATION	REFERENCE MANUAL	CODING	CHECKOUT	SYSTEM INTEGRATION

	INTERNAL SYSTEM SPEC		FLOWCHARTS		
C	B	A	C	B	A

. . .

JOBₖ

NAME	FUNCTIONAL SPECIFICATION	REFERENCE MANUAL	CODING	CHECKOUT	SYSTEM INTEGRATION

	INTERNAL SYSTEM SPEC		FLOWCHARTS		
C	B	A	C	B	A

MONTHLY REPORT

PROJECT NAME

DATE

(Note: The headings given in this report
model are not considered to be
all inclusive.   They should be
regarded by the user as changeable,
augmentable, etc. at his discretion.
The entire model should be viewed
as a plateau from which he may
want to proceed to prepare a
complete report specifically
geared to his project and its
reporting requirements.)

TABLE OF CONTENTS

I. INTRODUCTION

A brief orientation: project responsibility should be defined and some historical background given. Some information may be similar to that given in previous monthly reports; other information should be peculiar to this month's report.

II. STATUS OF THE PROJECT

Briefly verbalize the state of the project at this point in time. Reference past PROJECT WEEKLY REPORTS and the PROJECT HISTORICAL RECORD. It is important to call the reader's attention to the degree to which progress corresponds to that expected in the WORK PLAN and last month's projection.

III. WORK PLAN CONFORMANCE

This section should be similar in appearance to that of the WORK PLAN. Discuss every target date. If the original estimates were incorrect, present feasible ones in their place and remark on the cause for the change.

IV. ACCOMPLISHMENTS THIS MONTH

List all significant accomplishments realized during the reporting period this report covers.

V. ANTICIPATED ACCOMPLISHMENTS FOR COMING MONTH

Discuss projections appearing in the charts. Justify the projections.

VI. REMARKS

Discuss any item of an unusual nature not covered in the above section.

VII. PROJECT WEEKLY REPORTS

	FUNCTIONAL SPECIFICATION	REFERENCE MANUAL	INTERNAL SYSTEM SPEC ( )	FLOWCHARTS ( )	CODING	SYSTEM INTEGRATION
This month's progress and projections						

This month's progress stated as in thé PROJECT WEEKLY REPORTS. Next month's progress shown in weekly increments from the current week, k , through project weeks $k+1$, $k+2$, $k+3$, $k+4$.

	FUNCTIONAL SPECIFICATION	REFERENCE MANUAL	INTERNAL SYSTEM SPEC ( )	FLOWCHARTS ( )	CODING	SYSTEM INTEGRATION
Last month's progress and projections						

VIII. PROJECT HISTORICAL RECORD

JOB$_1$

NAME	FUNCTIONAL SPECIFICATION	REFERENCE MANUAL	CODING	CHECKOUT	SYSTEM INTEGRATION
	INTERNAL SYSTEM SPEC			FLOWCHARTS	
C	B	A	C	B	A

JOB$_2$

NAME	FUNCTIONAL SPECIFICATION	REFERENCE MANUAL	CODING	CHECKOUT	SYSTEM INTEGRATION
	INTERNAL SYSTEM SPEC			FLOWCHARTS	
C	B	A	C	B	A

...

JOB$_k$

NAME	FUNCTIONAL SPECIFICATION	REFERENCE MANUAL	CODING	CHECKOUT	SYSTEM INTEGRATION
	INTERNAL SYSTEM SPEC			FLOWCHARTS	
C	B	A	C	B	A

IX. CONCLUSION

Sum up the finding of this report with special emphasis on anticipated progress. Be brief.

G. SAMPLE DISPLAYS

The displays to be described in this section represent three basic ways of keeping the programming department's workload, staffing, project status, etc. before the departmental staff and others who may be interested. Also, the displays will be an invaluable aid to departmental management and the management of the department.

All the displays shown are easy to construct. Magnetized boards and associated item kits will suffice.* A sticky-plastic-tape, raised-printing kit can be used to produce all names, labels, etc.** The tape is stuck on the items included with the magnetized board.

Finally, a Polaroid camera can be used to record the displayed data.

1. The project status board.

    This board appears very much like the WEEKLY REPORT. Its format is on the next page.

---

*Sometimes called magnetic visual control systems.

**Produced with a DYMO (embossing tool) TAPEWRITER made by DYMO Products Company, Berkeley, California.

CHART 1
PROJECT STATUS CONTROL BOARD

Activity / Project	FUNC-TIONAL SPEC	REFER-ENCE MANUALS	INTERNAL SYSTEM SPEC( )	FLOW-CHARTS ( )	CODING	CHECKOUT	SYSTEM INTEGRA-TION	PERCENT COM-PLETED
PROJECT$_1$								
PROJECT$_2$								
PROJECT$_3$								
$\cdots$								
PROJECT$_n$								

NOTES:

- This board is maintained on a weekly basis by use of data from the PROJECT WEEKLY REPORTS. The rules for posting are exactly those used for the reports discussed in Section C, "The Personnel Reporting Procedure."

- Color coding of number tags can indicate work which is behind, on, or ahead of schedule (dates should exist in a WORK PLAN).

- The PERCENT COMPLETED column represents a figure which may be derived as given on page 11, this report.

111

2. Personnel versus time.

This display shows the allocation of staff (grouped according to project) over time. It appears as follows:

CHART 2

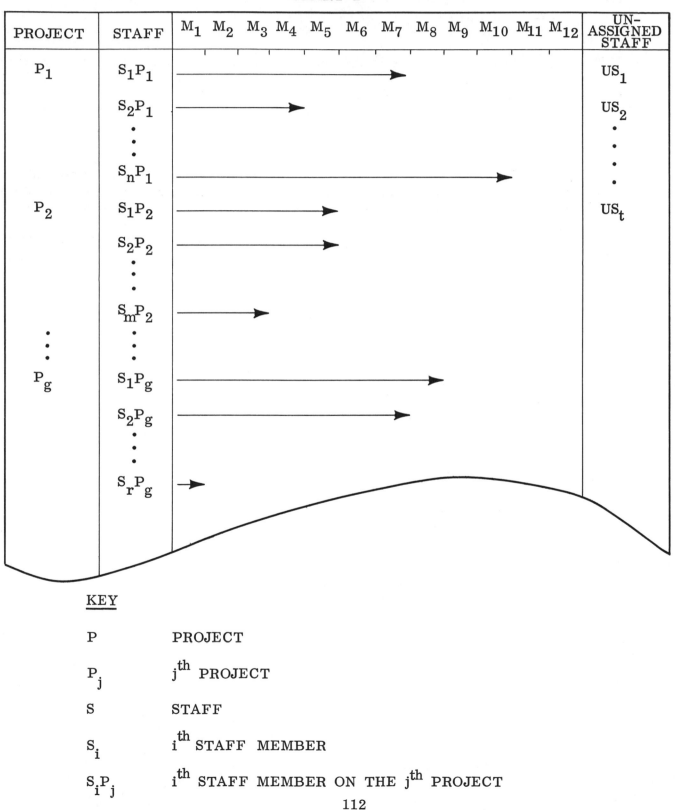

KEY

P	PROJECT
P_j	j^{th} PROJECT
S	STAFF
S_i	i^{th} STAFF MEMBER
$S_i P_j$	i^{th} STAFF MEMBER ON THE jth PROJECT

112

U	UNASSIGNED
US_k	k^{th} UNASSIGNED STAFF MEMBER
M	MONTH
M_h	h^{th} MONTH

NOTES:

- The number of months shown may vary. In the example display 12 are shown.

- The first month M_1 should be updated each month; hence all month labels shift to the left monthly.

- The arrows show the length of time each STAFF MEMBER is obligated to his PROJECT.

3. Project data and plans.

This display has a plastic envelope approximately four-by-four inches upon which key project data are kept (see card format below display) and a total time to completion projection as of a given reporting date.

CHART 3

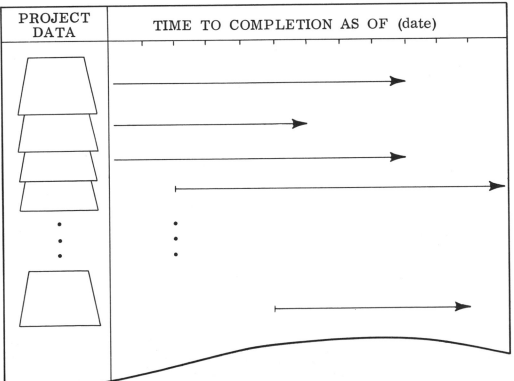

113

The format of the key project-data card is as follows:

PROJECT NAME	STARTING DATE
MANAGER	ENDING DATE
USER	BUDGET

REMARKS

(List all significant events such as changes, suspension, delays, achievements, etc. as numbered items, much the same as a doctor would keep a patient's record.)

NOTES:

- Color coding can signify lateness, ahead of schedule conditions, etc.

- The cards should be filed and kept as part of the project history after project completion.

CHECKLIST FOR
PROGRESS REPORTING

	YES	NO
Is a progress report subdivided into several categories? (See Section C, above, "The Personnel Reporting Procedure.")	☐	☐
Is the distinction between C-level, B-level, and A-level documentation clear to the EXTERNAL GROUP?	☐	☐
Are WEEKLY REPORTS submitted at the programmer level?	☐	☐

Does the programming project leader summarize these reports:

	YES	NO
• Weekly?	☐	☐
• Monthly?	☐	☐
Is the PROJECT MONTHLY REPORT closely tied to the WORK PLAN in outline?	☐	☐
Does it reference the WORK PLAN liberally?	☐	☐
Is a PROJECT HISTORICAL RECORD kept?	☐	☐
When chart summarization takes place, are weighting factors used with care?	☐	☐

VII. Programming Communications

A. INTRODUCTION

In an organization having a hierarchical structure, communication can be classified into two broad categories: that which passes from one level of employee to another and that which does not. An example of the first is the MONTHLY PROGRESS REPORT issued by a group leader to his superiors; an example of the second is an intergroup memo noting changes to a program interface.

These categories of information can be further characterized by the degree of formality involved in their preparation. A document destined to pass through one or more levels of management, as the MONTHLY PROGRESS REPORT will, takes on an official quality not present in an intergroup report or memo.

This does not imply that "official" documents need be difficult to organize and prepare; furthermore, it does not imply that working papers need be imprecise.

Much of the material in this book is devoted to the simplification of formal reporting. The chapters on "Work Plan Preparation," "Time and Cost Estimating," and "Progress Reporting" provide outlines which insure completeness and ease of preparation.

One aim of the skeletal outlines included in this and other parts of the book is to reduce the work of both the originator and the recipients of a document by eliminating unnecessary verbiage.

Another aim is to insure accuracy by directing the author's thoughts along pre-established paths known by past experience to require documenting. The intergroup reporting procedure presented herein provides this direction without introducing undue formality into the day-to-day office environment.

The format of this chapter reflects the distinction made above with regard to information classes. In "Formal Document Flow" a review of the definition and intent of each report shown in the project enactment charts is made, and its author and recipients are identified. The section entitled "Intergroup Correspondence" is a formalization of communication procedures to be followed by programming personnel in performing a group effort.

B. FORMAL DOCUMENT FLOW

The organization of this section was suggested by the PROJECT ENACTMENT flowchart appearing in the Introduction--that is, a phase-by-phase definition of information flow described in pictorial form. Each phase of the project shown in the enactment chart is represented.

In addition a separate paragraph is devoted to PROGRESS REPORT distribution. Because PROGRESS REPORTING takes place continually throughout the project, it cannot be identified with any one phase.

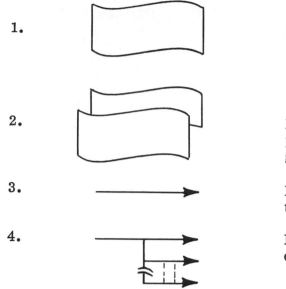

1.   Denotes a document.

2.   Denotes two documents produced in parallel by a common author or group.

3.   Denotes the routing of a document to a single individual.

4.   Denotes the routing of a document or documents to many individuals.

5.   Often, a document will pass through channels. This is indicated by a single arrow pointing to the initial recipient. The subsequent recipients are listed below the first, as shown in the following example:

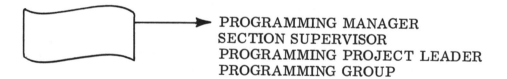

PROGRAMMING MANAGER
SECTION SUPERVISOR
PROGRAMMING PROJECT LEADER
PROGRAMMING GROUP

In this case the EXTERNAL FUNCTIONAL SPECIFICATION is first received by the programming manager, who passes it on to the section supervisor, who assigns the document to a programming project leader, who finally distributes it to his staff.

6.   Where possible, the relative time of the appearance of documents is indicated by a vertical time axis (increasing time is from top to bottom). Due to the constraint of page size, parallel development is not always shown. When this occurs, a note indicating the true time relationship will be appended to the diagram.

ANALYSIS PHASE

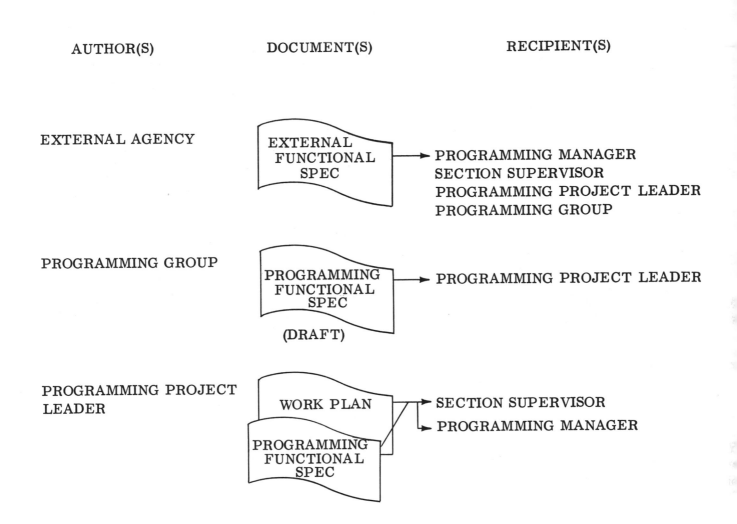

ALPHA REVIEW

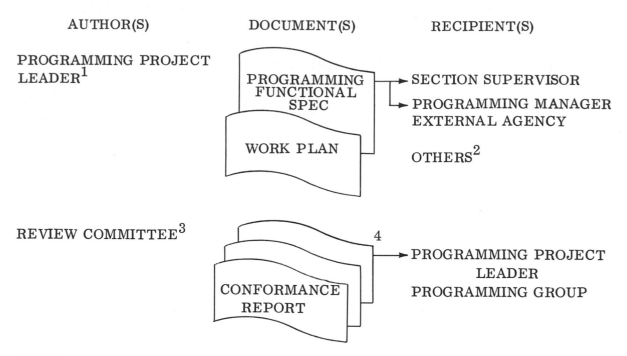

AUTHOR(S)	DOCUMENT(S)	RECIPIENT(S)

PROGRAMMING PROJECT LEADER[1]

PROGRAMMING FUNCTIONAL SPEC

WORK PLAN

→ SECTION SUPERVISOR
→ PROGRAMMING MANAGER
EXTERNAL AGENCY

OTHERS[2]

REVIEW COMMITTEE[3]

CONFORMANCE REPORT [4]

→ PROGRAMMING PROJECT LEADER
PROGRAMMING GROUP

NOTES:

[1]This step repeats the last step shown for the DESIGN PHASE, with one exception: the distribution of the documents to other interested parties. This distribution does not take place during design. Management may be interested in reviewing early versions of the programming project leader's work and advising him during preliminary stages. The DESIGN PHASE chart emphasizes this.

[2]Members of the review committee to be appointed by the programming manager.

[3]The programming manager, section supervisor, programming project leader, EXTERNAL AGENCY representatives, and those invited from the PROGRAMMING DEPARTMENT.

[4]This report may simply be minutes of the review meeting along with any relevant memos produced by those in attendance. If the design is acceptable at this point, the report must contain, in effect, a signature of approval by the EXTERNAL AGENCY representative.

DESIGN PHASE

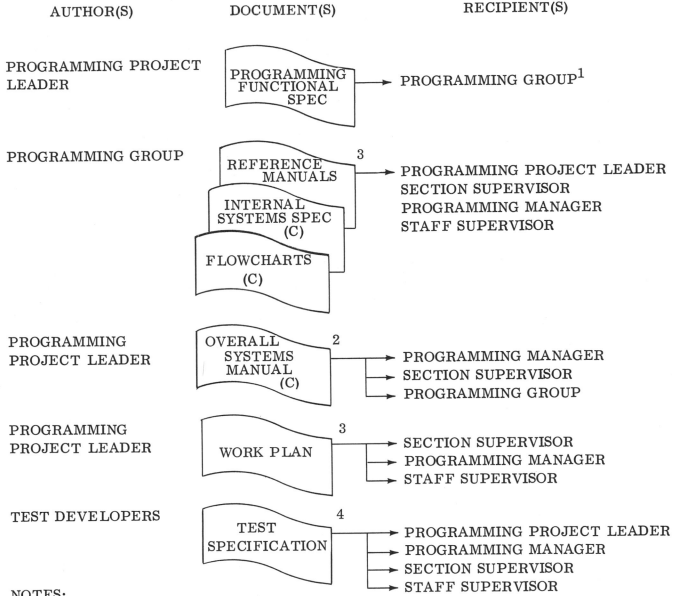

AUTHOR(S)	DOCUMENT(S)	RECIPIENT(S)
PROGRAMMING PROJECT LEADER	PROGRAMMING FUNCTIONAL SPEC	→ PROGRAMMING GROUP[1]
PROGRAMMING GROUP	REFERENCE MANUALS [3] INTERNAL SYSTEMS SPEC (C) FLOWCHARTS (C)	→ PROGRAMMING PROJECT LEADER SECTION SUPERVISOR PROGRAMMING MANAGER STAFF SUPERVISOR
PROGRAMMING PROJECT LEADER	OVERALL SYSTEMS MANUAL (C) [2]	→ PROGRAMMING MANAGER → SECTION SUPERVISOR → PROGRAMMING GROUP
PROGRAMMING PROJECT LEADER	WORK PLAN [3]	→ SECTION SUPERVISOR → PROGRAMMING MANAGER → STAFF SUPERVISOR
TEST DEVELOPERS	TEST SPECIFICATION [4]	→ PROGRAMMING PROJECT LEADER → PROGRAMMING MANAGER → SECTION SUPERVISOR → STAFF SUPERVISOR

NOTES:

[1] In all probability the programming group has expanded. Those taking part in the DESIGN PHASE form the core of the project. New members will have to familiarize themselves with the specifications.

[2] This does not appear in the charts. It is an overview document explaining the general structure of the system. Included in this book is a section on every system interface and other considerations of a global nature. The OVERALL SYSTEMS MANUAL will be discussed further under Item C below, "Intergroup Communication."

[3] As in the DESIGN/DESIGN REVIEW cycle, management may consult various documents before a formal review takes place.

[4] The TEST SPECIFICATION is developed in parallel with the three documents created by the PROGRAMMING GROUP. Test criteria should be established by an independent team of programmers.

GAMMA REVIEW

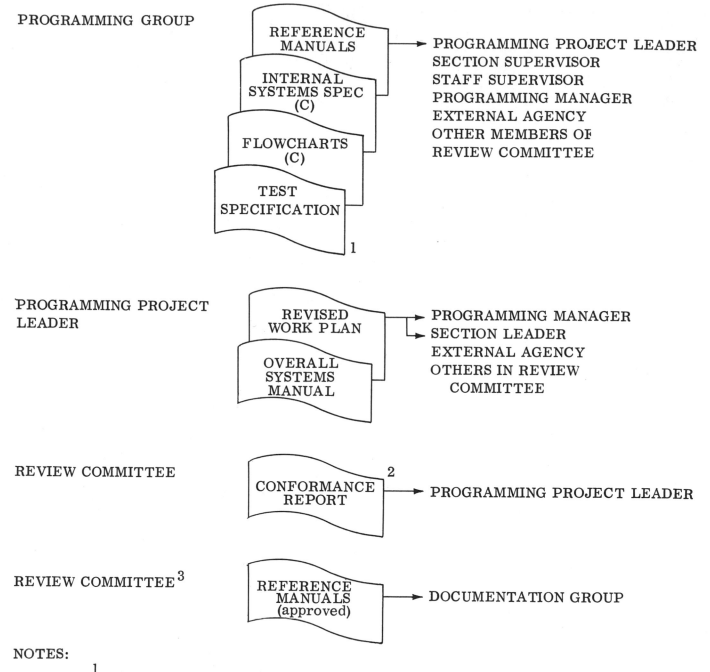

AUTHOR(S)	DOCUMENT(S)	RECIPIENT(S)

PROGRAMMING GROUP

REFERENCE MANUALS

INTERNAL SYSTEMS SPEC (C)

FLOWCHARTS (C)

TEST SPECIFICATION¹

→ PROGRAMMING PROJECT LEADER
SECTION SUPERVISOR
STAFF SUPERVISOR
PROGRAMMING MANAGER
EXTERNAL AGENCY
OTHER MEMBERS OF
REVIEW COMMITTEE

PROGRAMMING PROJECT LEADER

REVISED WORK PLAN

OVERALL SYSTEMS MANUAL

→ PROGRAMMING MANAGER
SECTION LEADER
EXTERNAL AGENCY
OTHERS IN REVIEW
COMMITTEE

REVIEW COMMITTEE

CONFORMANCE REPORT²

→ PROGRAMMING PROJECT LEADER

REVIEW COMMITTEE³

REFERENCE MANUALS (approved)

→ DOCUMENTATION GROUP

NOTES:

[1] Included to simplify this chart.

[2] This represents approval on the part of the EXTERNAL AGENCY (see ALPHA REVIEW Note 4).

[3] The review committee is the author of this book only in that it indicates approval of it. The document cannot be considered finished until the appropriate signatures are obtained.

CODING PHASE

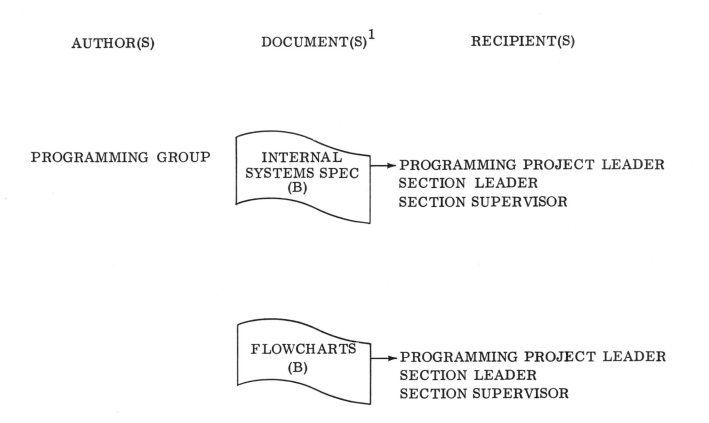

AUTHOR(S)   DOCUMENT(S)[1]   RECIPIENT(S)

PROGRAMMING GROUP   INTERNAL SYSTEMS SPEC (B)   →   PROGRAMMING PROJECT LEADER
                                                              SECTION LEADER
                                                              SECTION SUPERVISOR

                             FLOWCHARTS (B)   →   PROGRAMMING PROJECT LEADER
                                                              SECTION LEADER
                                                              SECTION SUPERVISOR

NOTE:

[1] A FIRST LISTING is shown in the PROJECT ENACTMENT CHART. This does not qualify as a formal document at this time. Eventually, however, a final listing will be produced that will be considered part of the internal systems manual.

DEBUG PHASE

AUTHOR(S)	DOCUMENT(S)	RECIPIENT(S)

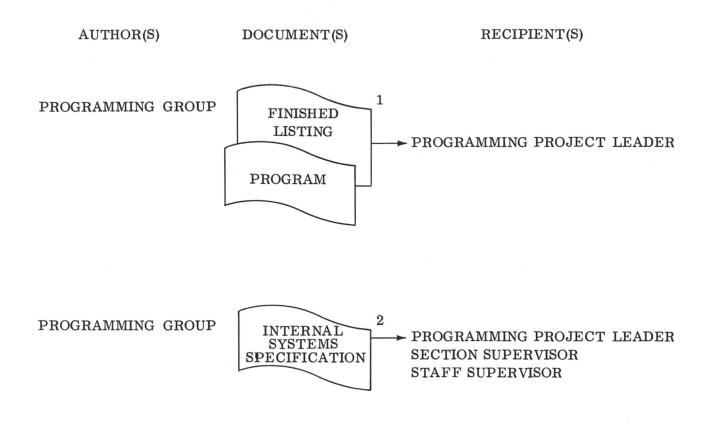

PROGRAMMING GROUP — FINISHED LISTING / PROGRAM [1] → PROGRAMMING PROJECT LEADER

PROGRAMMING GROUP — INTERNAL SYSTEMS SPECIFICATION [2] → PROGRAMMING PROJECT LEADER / SECTION SUPERVISOR / STAFF SUPERVISOR

NOTES:

[1] This listing, when correct, will be an appendix to the INTERNAL SYSTEMS SPECIFICATION.

[2] The INTERNAL SYSTEMS SPECIFICATION has the appearance of a finished document at this point in time. Every topic that will appear in the final edition is discussed. This is not to say that it is error free; small revisions may be made in the SYSTEM TEST phase and even during maintenance.

SYSTEM TEST PHASE

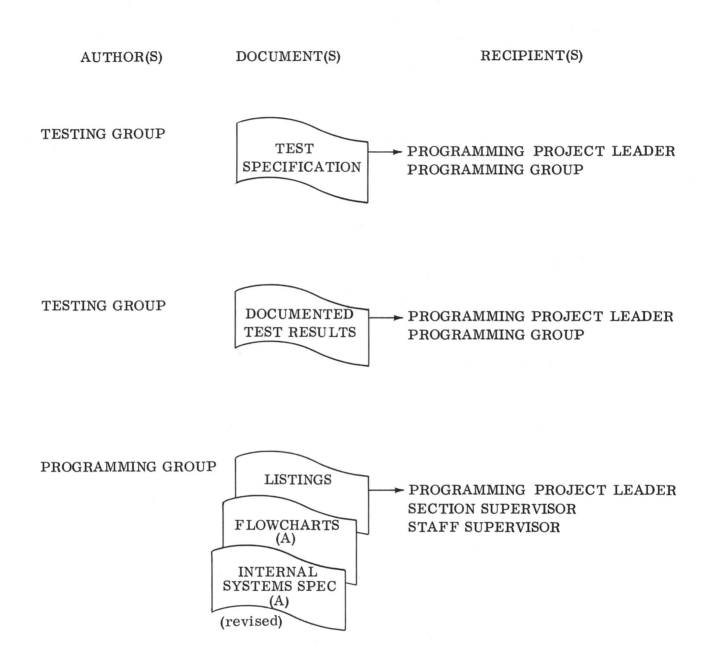

AUTHOR(S)	DOCUMENT(S)	RECIPIENT(S)
TESTING GROUP	TEST SPECIFICATION	PROGRAMMING PROJECT LEADER PROGRAMMING GROUP
TESTING GROUP	DOCUMENTED TEST RESULTS	PROGRAMMING PROJECT LEADER PROGRAMMING GROUP
PROGRAMMING GROUP	LISTINGS FLOWCHARTS (A) INTERNAL SYSTEMS SPEC (A) (revised)	PROGRAMMING PROJECT LEADER SECTION SUPERVISOR STAFF SUPERVISOR

ACCEPTANCE REVIEW

AUTHOR(S)   DOCUMENT(S)   RECIPIENT(S)

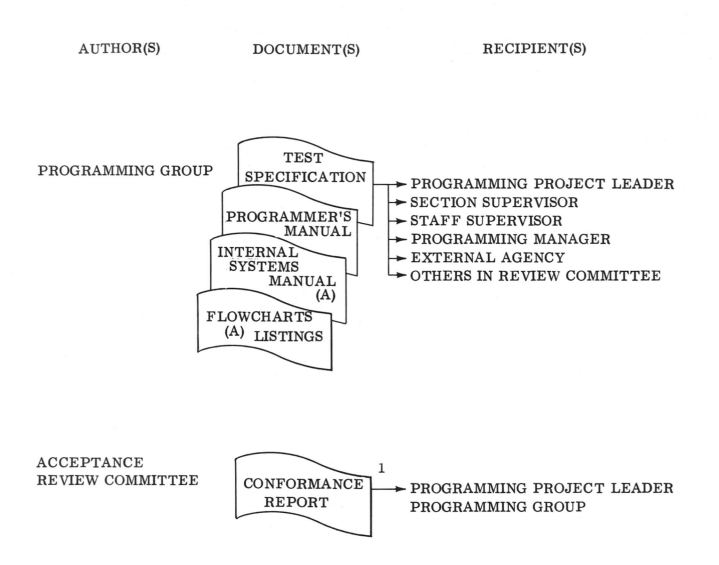

NOTE:

[1] Again, acceptance involves a signoff on the part of the EXTERNAL AGENCY.

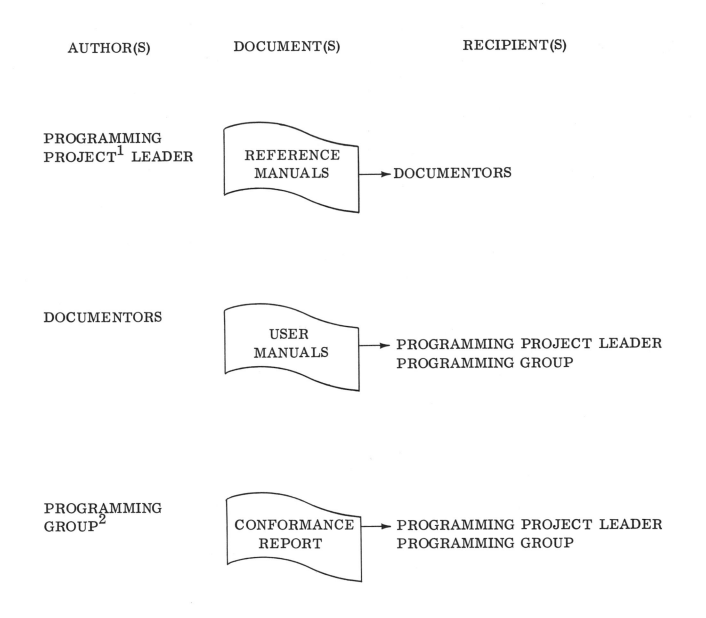

AUTHOR(S)	DOCUMENT(S)	RECIPIENT(S)
PROGRAMMING PROJECT[1] LEADER	REFERENCE MANUALS	DOCUMENTORS
DOCUMENTORS	USER MANUALS	PROGRAMMING PROJECT LEADER PROGRAMMING GROUP
PROGRAMMING GROUP[2]	CONFORMANCE REPORT	PROGRAMMING PROJECT LEADER PROGRAMMING GROUP

NOTES:

[1] The programming project leader is best described here as the author/ distributor of this material. Not all of the writing is his, although he is responsible for its content.

[2] Each individual programmer reviews the information familiar to him for <u>correctness</u>. Questions of style, presentation, etc. are reviewed by personnel outside the PROGRAMMING DEPARTMENT.

ACCEPTANCE PERIOD: MAINTENANCE AND MAINTENANCE GROUP TRAINING

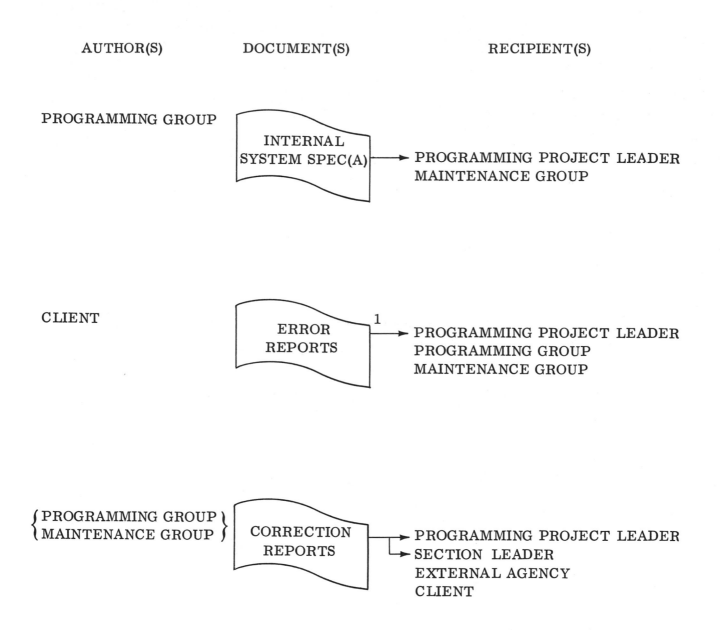

AUTHOR(S)   DOCUMENT(S)   RECIPIENT(S)

PROGRAMMING GROUP

INTERNAL SYSTEM SPEC(A) → PROGRAMMING PROJECT LEADER MAINTENANCE GROUP

CLIENT

ERROR REPORTS ¹→ PROGRAMMING PROJECT LEADER PROGRAMMING GROUP MAINTENANCE GROUP

{ PROGRAMMING GROUP MAINTENANCE GROUP }

CORRECTION REPORTS → PROGRAMMING PROJECT LEADER → SECTION LEADER EXTERNAL AGENCY CLIENT

NOTE:

[1] It is important that these reports be written so that they are useful to those maintaining the system. Forms should be provided to insure accurate reporting.

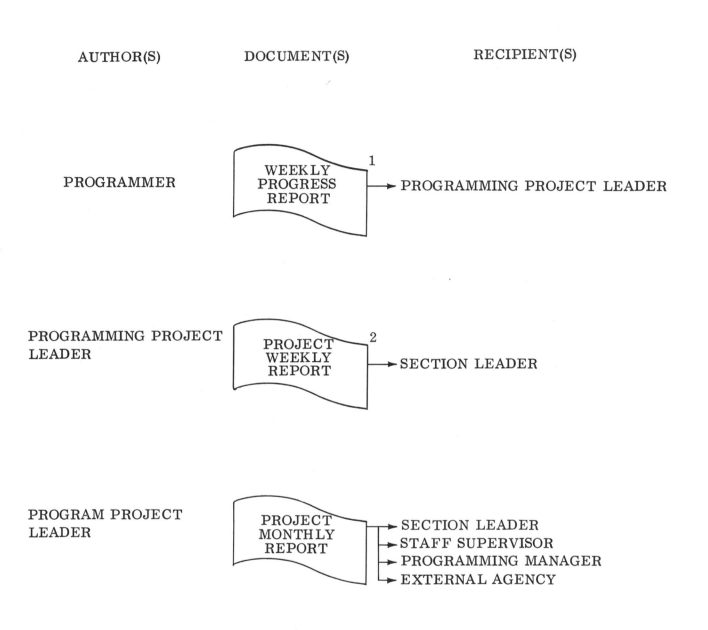

AUTHOR(S)	DOCUMENT(S)	RECIPIENT(S)
PROGRAMMER	WEEKLY PROGRESS REPORT [1]	→ PROGRAMMING PROJECT LEADER
PROGRAMMING PROJECT LEADER	PROJECT WEEKLY REPORT [2]	→ SECTION LEADER
PROGRAM PROJECT LEADER	PROJECT MONTHLY REPORT	→ SECTION LEADER → STAFF SUPERVISOR → PROGRAMMING MANAGER → EXTERNAL AGENCY

NOTES:

[1] A "fill in the blanks" report form. This report is distributed to the section leader as an appendix to the project leader's weekly report.

[2] One page of writing plus attachments.

C. INTERGROUP COMMUNICATION

Even though the atmosphere within a programming group ideally promotes free technical interchange, it is necessary to formalize the communication of information which might have global impact.

The OVERALL SYSTEMS MANUAL mentioned earlier in this chapter should contain a summary of all global identifiers, communication areas, and other important system interface definitions in a section called "System Interfaces." A first version of this summary should appear early in the DESIGN phase and must be maintained during the life of the project to incorporate changes as they occur.

The procedure by which changes to the OVERALL SYSTEMS MANUAL are put into effect is as follows:

- A programmer recognizes the need for some change.

- He consults with others in the group that he feels may be affected by the proposed revision.

- Provided he finds no opposition, the programmer completes a "Proposed Change" form and submits it to the group leader and section supervisor.

- If the programming project leader approves, the form is distributed throughout the group.

- If someone objects, a meeting is held between the objector(s), group leaders, section supervisor, and the author of the proposed change in which a compromise is negotiated.

- If a change is to be made, an approved "Proposed Change" form is issued by the section supervisor and group leader responsible.

- Revised editions of SYSTEM INTERFACES are issued weekly, if necessary.

The "Proposed Change" form appears below.

PROPOSED CHANGE

CHANGE

Identify the affected portions of the manual. Write the change as a set of replacement pages to the document.

REASON FOR CHANGE

IMPACT ON THE SYSTEM

List each component of the system thought to be affected by the change; identify the areas within SYSTEM INTERFACES that must be modified, and reword them.

CHECKLIST FOR
PROGRAMMING COMMUNICATIONS

	YES	NO
Does the EXTERNAL FUNCTIONAL SPECIFICATION provide an adequate basis for ANALYSIS?	☐	☐
Are parts of the PROGRAMMING FUNCTIONAL SPECIFICATION submitted to the programming project leader as they are completed?	☐	☐
Is the EXTERNAL FUNCTIONAL SPECIFICATION distributed along with the PROGRAMMING FUNCTIONAL SPECIFICATION?	☐	☐
Are all interested parties on the REVIEW COMMITTEE invited to contribute a section to the CONFORMANCE REPORT?	☐	☐
Is C-level documentation sufficiently detailed to allow CODING to begin?	☐	☐
Are REFERENCE MANUALS sufficiently complete and readable to allow an independent group of technical writers to develop USER MANUALS?	☐	☐
Does an explanatory note accompany all documents to be distributed, explaining what items (if any) are superseded?	☐	☐
Are rules of document distribution followed?	☐	☐
Is the OVERALL SYSTEMS portion of the INTERNAL SYSTEMS SPECIFICATION maintained by the programming project leader?	☐	☐
Are "Proposed Change" forms used to update the OVERALL SYSTEMS DESCRIPTION?	☐	☐
Are revised editions of the OVERALL SYSTEMS MANUAL issued weekly if changes occur?	☐	☐
Is a history of OVERALL SYSTEMS MANUAL changes kept for reference?	☐	☐

NOTES

NOTES

VIII. Documentation

A. INTRODUCTION

Documentation requirements reflect the recognition of the need for communication. The need for communication may be an immediate one--answered by those documents which are working input for study, coding, or some related activity. The need for communication may be a remote one--met by documents which are source material for comparing a current effort with past similar projects.

Timing, therefore, assumes major significance in the task of documenting. The utility of working documents depends on their being available. The reliability of historical documents depends upon their being written when information is current and complete.

All information documented during the course of a programming project shares yet another type of time dependence. Throughout the performance of a project there is constant maturation of product definition and enactment experience. Therefore, while documents of the same form dealing with a given aspect of the task appear at several stages, the depth of content varies greatly. As the product becomes more clearly defined, project documentation deepens in detail.

The evolution of product definition from the form of first specification to the finished system may be traced in project documents.   At each stage of development the information provided parallels the status of the enactment effort. There is no duplication of information; specifications produced during ANALYSIS, for example, are subsets of those produced during DESIGN. Any repetition of information is restricted to that which is necessary to insure clarity and continuity.

At each stage a body of documentation is generated which has immediate use as source material for the next stage and ultimate use as reference.   Content depth is related to both product definition and the purpose of the document. Specific document requirements at the several logical stages of enactment are listed on the PROJECT ENACTMENT CHART.

The discussion which follows describes the level and general nature of each of the documents shown on the charts. In addition the point within the applicable activity at which a given document should be prepared is indicated.

Format and specific content of programming project documentation are not the proper subjects of this book. Models should be devised for each document type to insure completeness as well as consistency and familiarity to facilitate both preparation and use. One example of such a model appears in Chapter II --"Work Plan Preparation."

B. CHARACTERISTICS OF DOCUMENTATION

In general there are four important characteristics which identify programming documentation:

- Completeness--no necessary details omitted.
- Economy--no superfluous verbiage used.
- Clarity--no jargon or esoteric language employed.
- Timeliness--no loss of working time when needed; no loss of information when prepared.

All documentation written during a programming project may be classified for discussion under one of the following headings:

- SPECIFICATIONS--e.g., EXTERNAL FUNCTIONAL SPECIFICATIONS, INTERNAL SYSTEM SPECIFICATIONS, TEST SPECIFICATIONS.
- REFERENCE MANUALS.
- PROGRAM LISTING.
- FLOW CHARTS.
- WORK PLANS.
- REPORTS--e.g., WEEKLY PROGRESS REPORTS, MONTHLY PROGRESS REPORTS, CONFORMANCE REPORTS.
- REFERENCES--e.g., REFERENCE MANUALS, USER'S MANUALS.
- PROMOTIONAL MATERIAL.

These general categories are, clearly, not mutually exclusive. The breakdown is made along lines which allow for the best treatment of specific items. A WORK PLAN, for example, might be classified as a report but is of sufficient importance to be treated separately.

C. DOCUMENTING DURING ANALYSIS

All documents written in the ANALYSIS PHASE are broadly descriptive. They present the product in terms of its largest constituents. There are several classes of documents, all of the most general nature, prepared during ANALYSIS.

1. Specifications.

   A project begins when a programming FUNCTIONAL SPECIFICATION is given to programming personnel. It is derived from an EXTERNAL FUNCTIONAL SPECIFICATION. Both documents are broad design descriptions. Each of them outlines the product to be prepared and lists its properties and intents. The difference lies in orientation:

   - An EXTERNAL FUNCTIONAL SPECIFICATION describes a product envisioned as the means of achieving some processing purpose and states the desired characteristics of that product.

   - A PROGRAMMING FUNCTIONAL SPECIFICATION describes that same product in terms of its programming environment, restrictions, capabilities, and use.

2. Work plan.

The format and content of the initial WORK PLAN follows the model given in Chapter II. At this early stage in the enactment cycle there will be several areas for which information is unavailable. All shortcomings should be noted as such, with explanatory notes indicating the time at which they will be remedied.

3. Reports.

Two types of reports are produced during ANALYSIS. The first is a standard, defined-progress indicator; the second is an accumulation of descriptive items relating to product conformance.

4. Progress reports.

Two types of WEEKLY PROGRESS REPORTS are prepared each week from the first week of project enactment until completion. They are:

● WEEKLY REPORT.
● PROJECT WEEKLY REPORT.

The former is submitted by each member of the programming staff, giving an account of his activity on a preprinted form, and includes the following information:

● Current overall status.
● Work completed during the current week.
● Anticipated progress for the next week.
● Remarks.

The latter PROGRESS REPORT is a summary of the various PROGRESS REPORTS with all relevant WEEKLY REPORTS included as attachments.

PROGRESS REPORTS submitted weekly form a diary of the project; their writing, therefore, spans its life. For ease of use, they are summarized in the PROJECT HISTORICAL RECORD.

In addition to the weekly PROGRESS REPORTS, a PROJECT MONTHLY REPORT is originated by the programming project leader to be submitted to higher management. This report contains this month's progress and in addition all progress anticipated for the next month.

5. Conformance reports.

Each logical stage terminates in a review which produces a CONFORMANCE REPORT. At the end of ANALYSIS this is a collection of plans, specifications, and notes which tell whether or not the proposed product meets the originator's specifications in all aspects. Those areas in which the proposed system is less than the ideal are annotated, and the proposed compromise measures described.

All CONFORMANCE REPORTS include any intermediate evaluations, proposals, specifications, and the like which were refined and modified to produce the final versions. They are, therefore, development records showing the motivations for decisions taken during the enactment cycle.

Figure 3, which follows, is a checklist of documentation produced during the ANALYSIS activity.

D. DOCUMENTING DURING DESIGN/DEVELOPMENT/IMPLEMENTATION

Much the same sort of documentation is produced during DESIGN as is written during ANALYSIS. At this second stage, however, the skeletal descriptions which were given in earlier specifications and plans are fleshed out.

Another change in documentation occurs in DESIGN--the introduction of a new orientation. Most documents written during DESIGN are more internally oriented--i.e., they are designed for use by members of the programming staff. However, during DESIGN, user-oriented documentation is begun.

1. Internal system specifications (C).

   The PROGRAMMING FUNCTIONAL SPECIFICATION written during ANALYSIS forms the basis for specifications which are meticulously detailed descriptions of the purposes, techniques, restrictions, requirements, and rules of use of the proposed product-- the INTERNAL SYSTEMS SPECIFICATIONS (C). These latter blueprint the product in all its characteristics and properties and constitute its definitive description. INTERNAL SYSTEMS SPECIFICATIONS (C) are the source materials from which the system is coded.

   The INTERNAL SYSTEMS SPECIFICATIONS are the guide to implementation.

   A parallel set of specifications--THE TEST SPECIFICATIONS-- are written as an ongoing activity during basic DESIGN. Their purpose is to provide a complementary picture of the product system from the viewpoint of expectation of performance. TEST SPECIFICATIONS outline an extensive set of procedures designed to make an exhaustive inventory of system rules, capabilities, roquircmcnts, and results. When they are complete, tests may be implemented. Testing techniques may require some programs to be written--e.g., to check out a language processor. Or they may require only the creation of test problems.

FIGURE 3   DOCUMENTS WRITTEN DURING ANALYSIS

Document	Origin	Use
EXTERNAL FUNCTIONAL SPECIFICATIONS	Agency requesting project	Basic design reference material
PROGRAMMING FUNCTIONAL SPECIFICATIONS	Technical programming staff	1. Programming-oriented design description 2. Source document for detailed description of product to be developed
WEEKLY REPORTS	Programming staff	Enactment control
PROJECT WEEKLY REPORTS	Programming project leader	Enactment control
MONTHLY PROGRESS REPORTS	Programming project leader	Enactment control and planning
WORK PLANS	Programming project leader	Enactment control and planning
CONFORMANCE REPORT	Technical and management staff	Enactment control; product control

2. <u>Flowcharts (C)</u>.

Detailed implementational FLOWCHARTS (C) depend directly on the draft of the INTERNAL SYSTEMS SPECIFICATIONS (C) and are written from it. FLOWCHARTS generated as the product analysis is carried out are step-by-step directives for the procedure by which the product system is achieved. Every process in the sequence of operations which is necessary for realizing the aim of the system appears in its applicable program FLOWCHART.

Implementation FLOWCHARTS translated the INTERNAL SYSTEMS SPECIFICATIONS into the series of procedures which meet them.

When TEST SPECIFICATIONS show programs as items of TEST material, similar FLOWCHARTS are prepared for those programs. Every flowchart written during analysis is implementation-oriented and is the basis for the specific coded program written for the product computing environment.

3. <u>References</u>.

Once specified, a system is determined. Its characteristics are defined and the rules of its use can be formulated. One form of narrative reference appears in FLOWCHART statements. Another appears in user documentation. <u>User documentation is prepared by a professional technical writing staff.</u> Source material for that documentation is provided by the REFERENCE MANUALS, which are written from INTERNAL SYSTEMS SPECIFICATIONS and FLOWCHARTS and expanded, if necessary, during coding.

INTERNAL SYSTEMS SPECIFICATIONS (C) and detailed FLOW-CHARTS (C) imply a system context definition. This definition allows for the listing of requirements and expectations of use. A narrative description of the product along with rules of use and any restrictions is prepared by the programmer in the course of detailed analysis for implementation. Control record formats, interactions with existent systems, and the like are noted according to the model which applies to the system in preparation. Any coding- or hardware-dependent information, which in all cases is greatly minimized, is omitted with a note to the writing group indicating its omission. The REF-ERENCE MANUALS--i.e., the product documents* written by the programmer--are then submitted to the technical documentation department which writes the user documents.

As coding is carried out and test techniques are developed, any new information that is applicable is submitted to the documenting staff to complement the original material.

---

* PROGRAMMER REFERENCE and OPERATIONS REFERENCE.

Preparation of final user documentation is not a function of the programming staff and not, therefore, properly a topic for discussion in this book.

The responsibility of the programming group is that of providing complete, accurate, clear information as soon as it is possible to do so and of reviewing the technical content of finished documents.

The REFERENCE MANUALS provide sufficient information for writing user documents for user release.

4. Listings.

Coding begins when implementation FLOWCHARTS are complete. As soon as the keypunching service returns cards punched from the programming forms for a program, those forms are used to check the listing of the punched cards. The programming sheets are then discarded. Programming sheets are simple intermediate program documents and never a permanent part of project files.

PROGRAM LISTINGS are transient forms until system release.

There is one LISTING extant at all times--the output of the most recent processing of the source program. A LISTING is valid until a new one is produced. At that time the prior LISTING becomes obsolete and is discarded. The current working version of the program LISTING is used to record changes to the source program. It serves, by means of comment material, to cross-reference the FLOWCHARTS. As each new LISTING is generated, corrections are made to the implementational FLOWCHARTS, if necessary, and the old LISTING is destroyed.

5. Internal system specifications (B) and (A).

As the requisite information emerges from program analysis, coding, and testing experience, the programmer writes his INTERNAL SYSTEMS SPECIFICATIONS (B) and (A). Like all other documentation prepared by the programmer, this is done as an ongoing part of his implementation task.

The B and A versions of this specification are amplifications upon and corrected versions of the C-level document.

6. Reports.

The standard reports continue to form part of the documentation task during CODING.

As debugging progresses, the programmer is in a position to make recommendations for the competencies desirable in the person chosen to maintain his program. These recommendations are included in the WEEKLY and MONTHLY PROGRESS REPORTS for communication to management.

7. Conformance reports.

The CONFORMANCE REPORTS produced during the implementation stage follow widely spaced review functions. At the completion of detailed analysis and specifications, two review functions take place.

The first review held during the DESIGN/DEVELOPMENT/IMPLE-MENTATION stage is a technically oriented one--the BETA REVIEW. The CONFORMANCE REPORT contains evaluations of the compatibility of detailed flowcharts and specifications with the preliminary design descriptions, along with evaluations of planned testing and user procedures. Areas of compromise are annotated. Discrepancies are recorded, and the means taken to remedy them are described.

All planned techniques approved on the technical level have their consequent effects on resource utilization. This is the matter for the GAMMA REVIEW COMMITTEE to consider. The CONFORM-ANCE REPORT issued at this session is a complement to the technical report.

As is the case with all such reports, it is a collection of notes, proposals, counterproposals, decisions, and minutes of meetings that were held to discuss the product.

CONFORMANCE REPORTS are accumulated throughout the activity to which they apply. They are completed when all project sections have made the transition to the activity which follows the review function at which the report was originally issued.

Conformance is on many levels--to design standards, implementational excellence, anticipated resource utilization, and product intent. A product may be accepted for release even though it does not conform ideally in some one respect.

8. Work plans.

Revised WORK PLANS are prepared during the implementation stage of enactment. None are, of course, new documents. Rather, each is a corrected version of the preceding WORK PLAN and reflects experience gained since the first was written. More information is included in several areas. Duration, expected resource utilization through to project termination, and expected effect of external factors can be more precisely predicted.

Figure 4 is a checklist of documentation during the DESIGN/ DEVELOPMENT/IMPLEMENTATION activities.

FIGURE 4   DOCUMENTS WRITTEN DURING DESIGN/DEVELOPMENT/
IMPLEMENTATION

Document	Origin	Use
INTERNAL SYSTEM SPECIFICATIONS (C), (B), (A)	Programming staff	1. Immediate source material for flowcharting 2. Reference material as part of the INTERNAL SYSTEMS MANUAL
TEST SPECIFICATIONS	Programming staff	1. Immediate source material for flowcharting or other test procedure development 2. Reference material as part of the test system report
FLOWCHARTS (C), (B), (A)	Programming staff	1. Source documents for coding 2. Reference material for maintenance
REFERENCE MANUALS	Programming staff	1. Reference for programmers preparing test procedures 2. Reference for operations personnel 3. Source material for documentation staff producing user documents

Document	Origin	Use
PROGRAMMING SHEETS	Programming staff	Keypunch material--discarded after use
LISTINGS	Programming staff	1. Working documents; valid till a new assembly or compilation--then destroyed Used to note results of check runs and to indicate corrections 2. Source documents for FLOWCHART modifications 3. Final version, a reference for maintenance
INTERNAL SYSTEMS MANUAL	Programming staff	Reference for maintenance*
WEEKLY REPORTS	Programming staff	Enactment control
PROJECT WEEKLY REPORT	Programming project leader	Enactment control and planning
PROJECT MONTHLY REPORTS	Programming project leader	Enactment control and planning
CONFORMANCE REPORTS	Technical and management staff	Enactment control; product control
WORK PLAN	Programming project leader	Enactment control

---

* A composite of INTERNAL SYSTEMS SPECIFICATION (A), FLOWCHARTS (A), LISTINGS (final), and advice to maintenance personnel.

E. POST RELEASE DOCUMENTATION

Immediately after release there is a shakedown period of customer familiarization. Then the standard maintenance period begins. At this point all system documentation relative to planning and implementation is complete and current. It then becomes reference material.

New documentation at this stage is as follows:

1. Reports.

Two things are being evaluated at this stage: the original system and proposed alterations.

Evaluations of the system are written after review of error reports. The reality and gravity of the reported malfunction are used as guides in determining what area of the overall product may be flawed: design, implementation, or user documentation. Such reports serve for guides in future efforts.

Proposed changes are evaluated in terms of the system purposes and major use as well as costs. These reports serve for immediate decision-making guides in modification reviews.

2. References.

Error reports and their associated correction reports become part of the INTERNAL SYSTEMS MANUAL. Error reports are, quite naturally, supplied by the user. When they are processed, correction reports are written--even if the latter are trivial statements explaining apparent error. All such information forms part of the necessary product description used by the maintainers.

At the same time, the maintainer issues references in the form of corrections to any already existing system documentation which is affected by his work.

CHECKLIST FOR
DOCUMENTATION

	YES	NO
Is the WORK PLAN finished?	☐	☐
Does the WORK PLAN explicitly note the lack of information needed but not available?	☐	☐
Are the PROGRAMMING FUNCTIONAL SPECIFICATIONS finished?	☐	☐
Are WEEKLY REPORTS being done?	☐	☐
Are PROJECT WEEKLY REPORTS being done?	☐	☐
Are MONTHLY PROGRESS REPORTS being done?	☐	☐
Are WORK PLAN changes being prepared?	☐	☐
Does the INTERNAL SYSTEM SPECIFICATION (C) exist?	☐	☐
INTERNAL SYSTEM SPECIFICATION (B)?	☐	☐
INTERNAL SYSTEM SPECIFICATION (A)?	☐	☐
Do TEST SPECIFICATIONS exist?	☐	☐
Do FLOWCHARTS (C) exist?	☐	☐
FLOWCHARTS (B)?	☐	☐
FLOWCHARTS (A)?	☐	☐
Do Programmer-produced REFERENCE MANUALS exist?	☐	☐
● PROGRAMMER'S MANUALS?	☐	☐
● OPERATIONS MANUALS?	☐	☐
Do program LISTINGS exist?	☐	☐
Has the INTERNAL SYSTEMS MANUAL been prepared?	☐	☐
Is the technical writing staff producing USER MANUALS?	☐	☐
Has provision been made for handling changes?	☐	☐

NOTES

NOTES

IX. Flowcharting

A. INTRODUCTION

FLOWCHARTS detail and pictorialize the action of the system product or project enactment. They make a graphic and narrative statement of the analysis of the problem to be solved in terms of the steps which lead to a solution.

FLOWCHARTS serve two distinct purposes in the project enactment. They are an essential form of system documentation, and they are blueprints for the programming tasks. As part of the documentation, they serve to reflect the level and nature of the system and the summaries of the system action. As programming tools, FLOWCHARTS form the specifications for coding a given process.

Clarity and simplicity of presentation are the ultimate goals of a FLOWCHART representation. There is no unique standard for a formalization which will insure these qualities for every aspect of the system. The designer of a FLOWCHART must consider the eventual user and decide which format or formats will provide the clearest understanding of the system he intends to convey.

The format conventions discussed in this chapter are included in three parts:

- Narrative FLOWCHARTS.

- Decision table charts.

- USASI* standard graphics.

When selecting the best formats for his FLOWCHARTS, the designer should select the charts most suited for comprehension and straightforwardness of presentation.

- Decision table charts are most applicable where large numbers of decisions and varying actions require description.

- USASI standard graphics are best used to show information flow or input/output of files from varied media.

- Narrative FLOWCHARTS have general applicability. They reduce the need for verbalization in technical documents and have the added advantage of being easily maintained.

- Most applications require the use of more than one of the above-mentioned FLOWCHARTING systems.

The narrative FLOWCHART, which presents the logical flow in a narrative fashion, is best suited for describing the program product in a series of

---

* Formerly ASA.

views--from the general to the very specific detail. It combines a descriptive and a pictorial flow representation. FLOWCHART text is spare but complete, giving a thorough summary of the information at each process step.

To insure that the system is described completely and simply, the narrative FLOWCHART is prepared in varying levels of detail. The number of different charts required to give an accurate description of the system depends directly on the complexity of the system. A relatively intricate system lends itself to division and several levels of subdivision.

In determining the depth of subdivision needed for meaningful charts, one must keep in mind that the potential audience for technical material is primarily drawn from those who are not members of the implementation staff.

- Succeeding levels should be similar enough in detail to allow an easy transition from one to the other.

- The most detailed level must allow for an easy transition from the narrative to the program listing.

B. NARRATIVE FLOWCHART STRUCTURE

The structure of these charts combines simple descriptive with directive pointers to produce a readily understandable system abstract.

Careful consideration must be given to the nature of the language employed in the narrative. Although FLOWCHARTS are working papers and are subject to change during the course of a project, the designer must always bear in mind that the eventual user may have no innate "in" knowledge of the project. To this end the language must be conventional and jargon free. Any standard terminology familiar to potential readers is acceptable.

The use of machine-dependent language is avoided at all levels of charting. No operational notation is used. Data are described in familiar language.

1. Basic format.

Each step of the narrative is written out as a brief declarative or imperative statement. The statements are single spaced within the logical unit and are bound by margins of not less than two inches.

EXAMPLE:

```
Retrieve the first record of the inventory control file.

Add the basic cost of this record to the current base price.

Write the computed cost onto the updated control file.
```

A break in the sequence of processing may occur in the following ways:

- An unconditional transfer.

- A decision causing a conditional transfer.

- An entrance into a subroutine.

The first two situations are handled explicitly through the use of connectors.

The transfer to a subroutine is implicit and is noted by the narrative, which states that a particular sequence of instructions is <u>performed</u> at that point.

2. <u>Nesting.</u>

NARRATIVE FLOWCHARTS become more readable if they are produced in levels of increasing detail. The following diagram is included to illustrate the nesting concept.

3. <u>Connectors--usage rules.</u>

A connector is a line indicating a transfer of the sequence from one step to another, noncontiguous step.

- When the sequence takes place from a step on one page to a step on the same page, the connector is drawn on the left margin ending in an arrow at the terminal statement.

- If the sequence involves steps not on the same physical page, the connector is drawn in the right margin of the statement from which transfer is made. The line is drawn downward, ending in an arrow and a statement identifier.

- If more than one such offpage connector exists on the same page, the connectors should be drawn in graduated lengths for the sake of clarity.

4. <u>Statement identifiers</u> (see chart that follows).

Statement identifiers are numeric characters from one to four digits in length, which correspond to the suffix portion of the program identifier.

- Statement identifiers are assigned to statements to which references occur on other physical pages.

- Statement identifiers appear on the left margin just preceding the statement being referenced.

- Statement identifiers appear below the connector arrow emanating from the statement containing the reference.

DIAGRAM TO ILLUSTRATE
NESTING CONCEPT

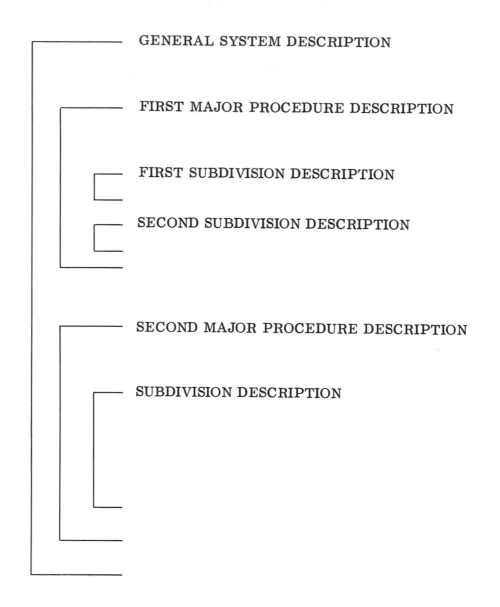

GENERAL SYSTEM DESCRIPTION

FIRST MAJOR PROCEDURE DESCRIPTION

FIRST SUBDIVISION DESCRIPTION

SECOND SUBDIVISION DESCRIPTION

SECOND MAJOR PROCEDURE DESCRIPTION

SUBDIVISION DESCRIPTION

NOTE: Divisions are not necessarily symmetric, nor is the number of divisions prescribed. These characteristics are determined by the nature of the system itself.

EXAMPLE: STATEMENT IDENTIFIERS

Page 1

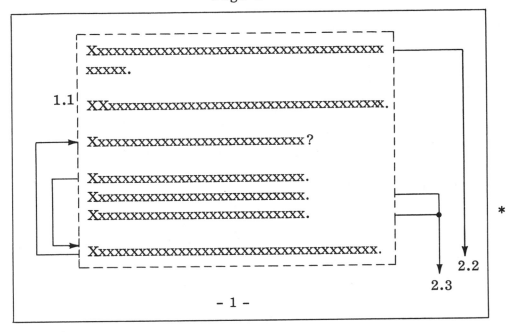

Page 2

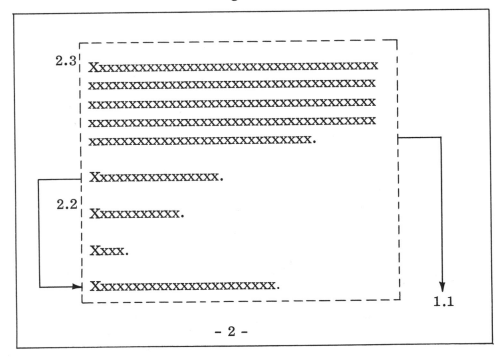

---

*Lines which cross but do not intersect in a dot have no common path.

- Statement identifiers are prefixed with the page number and a period. The page number refers to the page on which the referenced statement is physically located.

- If reference is made to a statement outside the program, the program code* must prefix the statement identifier.

- Duplicate statement identifiers are not allowed.

5. <u>Decision representation</u>.

Decision units must be grouped together with appropriate spacing. They should be typed on the same physical page.

EXAMPLE:

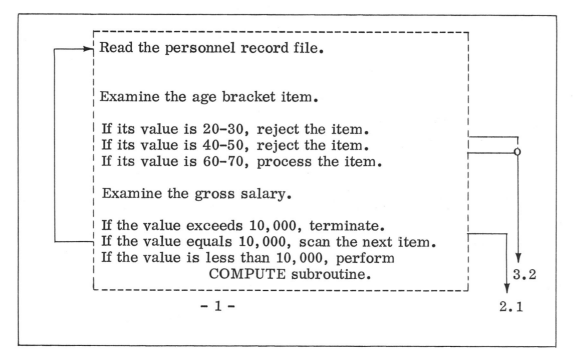

6. <u>Flowchart maintenance</u>.

Modifications to FLOWCHARTS are simply made. Insertions and deletions may be accomplished by cutting out the unwanted statements and pasting the remainder on a new page. It is then a relatively simple matter to draw new connectors.

- Retyping should be necessary only when the PROJECT END POINT is approaching.

---

*Each system component is assigned a two-letter identifying prefix (see Chapter X, "Coding").

- Intermediate copies--which may contain handwritten statements-- must be maintained in a legible form as project working documents.

Care must be taken to retain all linkages when a large number of statements must be inserted or if what was originally one page becomes two or more. Statements which were referenced by connectors may have to be referenced using offpage connectors.

7. Illustrative example.

To illustrate the use of multilevel narrative FLOWCHARTS, the following example is given.

Problem:

To find the smallest of n numbers in Table A. Table A is resident on an external file B. Place this number on external file C.

USE OF MULTILEVEL NARRATIVE FLOWCHART

Summary
Chart

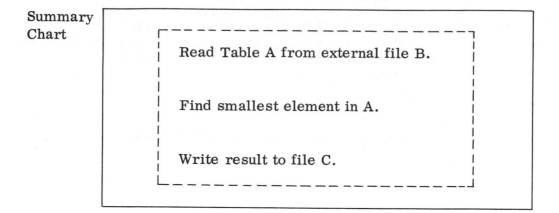

Read Table A from external file B.

Find smallest element in A.

Write result to file C.

Detailed
Chart

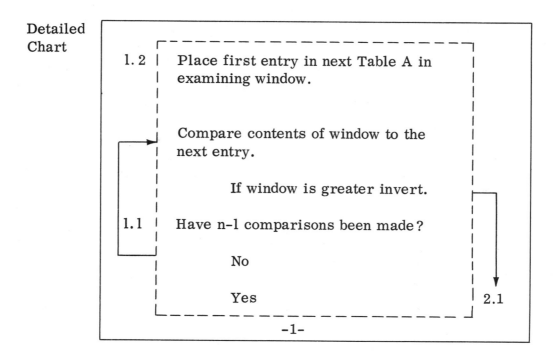

1.2 | Place first entry in next Table A in examining window.

Compare contents of window to the next entry.

If window is greater invert.

1.1 | Have n-1 comparisons been made?

No

Yes

2.1

-1-

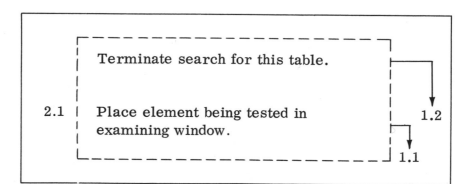

Terminate search for this table.

2.1 | Place element being tested in examining window.

1.2

1.1

C. DECISION TABLES

Decision table charting is a method designed to itemize large numbers of decisions, together with particular rules and associated actions, in a small, simplified pictorialization. This approach is effective in such runs as editing programs, scanning routines, etc.

The format of this type of charting is a rectangular figure, bordered by a vertical axis coordinate of the list of decisions and expressions and a horizontal axis coordinate of the rules which govern the decision processes. Each set of coordinates relates to a box within the major rectangle--which contains a $\underline{Y}$ (for Yes), an $\underline{N}$ (for No), or an $\underline{NA}$ (for Not Applicable), depending upon the relationship of the rule to the decision expression.

Each column in the chart defines a rule. To each rule there corresponds an action; this is indicated by subscript notation--i.e.:

$$\text{Rule (n)} \longleftrightarrow \text{Action (n)}$$

EXAMPLE:

RULES

DECISIONS	(1)	(2)	(3)	(4)
$A > B$	Y	Y	Y	N
C (alphabetic?)	N	NA	N	N
$M < 6$	Y	Y	N	Y
$N = 8$	Y	N	Y	NA

Action (1)   Xxxxxxxxxxxxxxxxxxxxxxxx.
                    xxxxxxx.

Action (2)   Xxxxxxxxxxxxxx.

Action (3)   Xxxxxxxxxxxxxxxx.
                    Xxxxxxx.
                    Xxxxxxxxxxx.

Action (4)   Xxxxxxxxxxxxxxxx.

                    Xxxxxxxxxxx.

D. USASI STANDARD GRAPHICS

It is assumed that the reader has a familiarity with the USASI-specified graphic notations.

The standard graphics provide an excellent overview of the system. Specifically, this type of charting provides a picture of the following:

- Information processing of the entire system.

- Documentation flow.

- Input/output files of the system.

- Overall project enactment.

These charts provide the maximum effectiveness when drawn on as few separate physical pages as possible. The number of boxes used is kept to a minimum. Accompanying narrative is sparse and is meant to supplement the boxed notation. In any case narrative is kept conventional and jargon free.

CHECKLIST FOR
FLOWCHARTING

	YES	NO
Is the language employed in flowcharts jargon free?	☐	☐
Is terminology used in NARRATIVE FLOWCHARTS standardized where possible?	☐	☐
Is the language used machine independent?	☐	☐
Does pointer and connector construction comply with the established standards?	☐	☐
Are statement identifiers from one to four digits long?	☐	☐
Are all offpage pointers graduated in length?	☐	☐
Are flowcharts on standard eight and one-half by 11-inch paper with reasonable margins?	☐	☐
Are decision groups set apart?	☐	☐
Are flowcharts prepared in gradual levels of detail?	☐	☐
Are the project-level conventions established for the FLOWCHARTS natural and simple to implement?	☐	☐
Can the FLOWCHARTS be readily used as a segment of the program documentation?	☐	☐
Are DECISION TABLES and USASI STANDARD GRAPHICS employed to supplement NARRATIVE FLOWCHARTS?	☐	☐
Is the transition from highest- to lowest-level FLOWCHART and finally to the LISTING easily made?	☐	☐

NOTES

X. Coding

A. INTRODUCTION

The coded program consists of those instructions necessary to accomplish the specifications as defined by the FLOWCHARTS. To simplify correlation of the logical flow between the CHARTS and the code, a set of conventions must be established and used by the programming staff.

Some obvious advantages to coding conventions include ease in:

- Debugging a segment of code.
- Maintenance and modification functions.
- Interfacing independent routines.

In the following discussion those elements of a coding on which conventions may be applied as well as coding techniques which should be avoided will be enumerated.

The conventions presented are to be considered a basis from which the reader can construct others geared to individual languages.

B. GENERAL DISCUSSION

The following are among the elements and methods for which guidelines will be drawn.

(1) Identifying labels representing:

- Location points.
- Constants.
- Variables.
- Global and local descriptive names.
- Macro and subroutine calls.

(2) Program and segment identification.

(3) Linkage procedures.

(4) Frequently used routines.

(5) Macro and subroutine structure.

(6) Comments and formats of the coded page.

(7) Coding techniques to avoid.

(8) Assembler and compiler tools.

(9) Programmer communications methods.

1. Identifying labels.

An identifying label must be constructed so that categorization and cross-referencing can be done with ease. In particular some concatenation of characters must be associated with a particular delineation of code.

Additional meaning is added to a rigid structure of standard labels when appropriate tools are built into the language processors.

Functionally, a label is identified with either of the following:

- A location or a table containing data.
- A location point in the stream of code.

For the purpose of standardization a label will be considered as a minimum of a seven-character field across language lines.

The first two characters of any label will represent a prespecified code associated with a segment of coding. These characters should be selected as a derivation of the segment name.

Data:

A data item can be constant or variable. It may be defined as a single item or as a resident of a table or array.

Character 3 of a label associated with data will provide the necessary information to specify its type.

Character 3 is: C if the label identifies a constant, or V if the label identifies a variable.

Character 4 may be made to designate the number of dimensions in an array or table where this concept is explicit.

The remaining three or four characters are left for the programmer's selection and must be unique. It is suggested that they be numeric and correspond to those specified in the FLOWCHARTS.

EXAMPLES:

SCC0113   Represents a constant in a routine called SCAN.

TGV2039   Represents a variable item in a routine such as TRIG. If this is defined in a higher level language, this item might be defined in a two-dimensional table.

Location points:

Location or branch point labels provide an easy means to cross-reference the coding, the FLOWCHART from which it was written, and indexing provided by the processor.

Character 3 is: L if the label is associated with a simple branch point, or M if the label is associated with a variable connector point.

Characters 4, 5, 6, and 7 are identical to the corresponding statement identifier specified in the FLOWCHART. If this identifier is fewer than four characters, the value is right-justified and zero-filled on the left.

At identifier 2.11, a test is made. The first branch point is out of the segment of coding to a global point in another routine (MXL006). The second transfer point is located within the coded routine itself. (See example below.)

2. Program and segment identification.

To simplify the task of integrating segments, macros, and routines into larger systems, associated names should be as descriptive as possible. The full seven-character label is reserved for a meaning-full mnemonic representation.

EXAMPLES:

LØGTABL
MØVDATA
SINCØSE

The first two characters are used for the standard prefix for any identifier within the given segment or program (see Item 1, above).

3. Linkage procedures.

Specific conventions cannot be created as a general case, since linkage is closely tied to the particular instructions available. However, each system should have such procedures carefully spelled out along the following lines:

xxxxxxxxxxxx Standard transfer instruction
-                    a Parameter information
-                    b

4. Frequently used routines.

Programmers should utilize certain standard routines. As an example, when a data movement or a character conversion is required, consider using a standard routine in place of an individually tailored one. (If no routine has been labeled standard, candidates for the title "standard routine" are routines known to be correct.) It is clear that debugging and documentation are facilitated when such a choice is made.

5. Macro and subroutine structure.

It is imperative that standard procedures be adopted with regard to the structure of subroutines and macro bodies (whenever the language itself does not demand such definition). Considerations are:

- Standard calls.

- Placement of descriptive "comments" (see below).

- Standard save procedures, where applicable.

- Placement of parameters.

6. Comments and formats.

A discussion of coding is incomplete without the inclusion of conventions for comments and formats which appear on the coded page. Comments must be considered as an integral part of the working program.

The first page must contain an introductory set of full-line comments preceding all routines. These comments will give the program name, date, modification number--if applicable--segment names, and a general functional description of the code that is to follow. In addition the call to this routine (if applicable) should be given--in precisely the format required--as well as the entry points and routines called by the code and all other relevant information. Methodology should be outlined.

Subheading comments should precede subsections of code where possible. These comments describe in more detail the function of the code that is to follow.

Individual lines of code should have associated with them detail-level comments. Although there need not be a one-to-one correspondence between comment and instruction, there should be such a correspondence between comment and the smallest delineation of function.

All areas, constants, variables, etc. should be documented by comments. Blank comment lines should be used to delineate logically independent routines.

EXAMPLE: RELATIONSHIP OF FLOWCHART AND LISTING

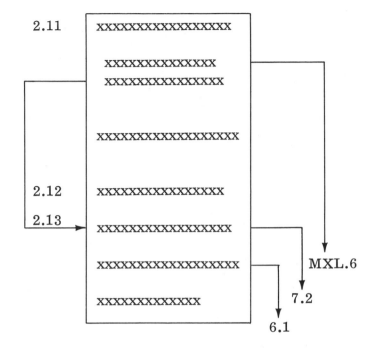

CODING (MOVE routine)

MØL0011	xxx	xxxxxxx
	xxx	MØL0006
	xxx	MØL0013
	xxx	xxxxxxx
MØL0012	xxx	xxxxxxx
MØL0013	xxx	MØL0002
	xxx	MØV0001
	xxx	xxxxxxx
	.	.
	.	.
	.	.
MØL0006	xxx	xxxxxxx
.	.	.
.	.	.
MØV0001	xxx	xxxxxxx
.	.	.
.	.	.
MØL0002	xxx	xxxxxxx

EXAMPLE: FIRST PAGE INCLUDING GENERAL COMMENT FORMATION

```
C      MØVE RØUTINE
C
C      FEBRUARY 1, 1967
C      MØDIFICATIØN  2
C
C      THIS RØUTINE MØVES THE CØNTENTS ØF A SPECIFIED
C      NUMBER ØF CELLS FRØM ØNE
C      SPECIFIED AREA TØ ANØTHER
C
C      CALL IS
C
C          xxxx        MØVE
C          xxxx        xxxxxx
C
C      PARAMETERS ARE . . .
C      RESTRICTIØNS ARE . . .
C      REFERENCES ARE . . .
C      METHODS USED ARE . . .
MØxxxxx    xxxx        xxxxxx          "EXPLAIN WHAT"
           xxxx        xxxxxx          "THE CØDING"
                 .           .         "DØES"
                 .           .
                 .           .
```

7. Techniques to avoid.

A frequent occurrence in programming is the discovery that a vital piece of coded information is totally incomprehensible. This can be inconsequential if the coding "works" and is totally isolated. More often, however, coding must be modified or integrated by individuals heretofore unfamiliar with the program. To facilitate the transfer of responsibility, the programmer originating the code must make the instruction pattern as simple and straightforward as possible, suppressing all urges to be "cute." That is not to say that techniques that save both time and space are to be curtailed. It is merely a question of weighing what is to be gained over the simplest possible approach. In particular a programmer should try to avoid:

- Instructions that become unrecognizably altered at object time.

- Multiple levels of nesting, if more direct methods are available and are as effective.

- Selection of nonmeaningful names--e.g., CAT, MAT.

- Relative addressing of the type:

    TRANSFER   AB00001 + 23

Insertion or deletion of instructions is bound to cause difficulties.

8. Assembler and compiler tools.

The language processor should be designed to provide an alphabetized index of all identifiers. This should include all reference and definition points between the listed items and corresponding relative addresses in the listing.

This will have the effect of grouping all constants, variables, and location points into distinct groups. Advantages are obvious for debugging, modifying, interfacing, and documenting purposes.

9. Programmer communication methods.

If it is necessary for the programmer to institute a change in some prespecified information of a global nature, and if he has the approval of all concerned, he must complete a PROPOSED-CHANGE form for submission to his GROUP LEADER and SECTION SUPERVISOR.

This would be necessary if, for example, a programmer wished to change the size of a communication area or to reserve an additional index register for certain system processing.

An example of such a change follows.

167

PROPOSED CHANGE

CHANGE

Communication area CØMMØN is to be increased from 400 to 405
locations. The additional five locations are to be added at the end
of the present area (i.e., after CØ00001 + 399). Each location will
contain pointer and word-count information.

REASON FOR CHANGE

Additional switches are needed for expanding snap-shot facilities
when in the system debug mode.

IMPACT ON THE SYSTEM

All processors providing system debug facilities must scan the
additional items.

CHECKLIST FOR
CODING

	YES	NO
Has the project code been established for label information?	☐	☐
Are the statement identifiers completely specified in the FLOWCHARTS?	☐	☐
Are linkage procedures defined?	☐	☐
Is there a compiled list of commonly used routines?	☐	☐
Have subroutine and macro structures been defined?	☐	☐
Does a full set of comments--to include program name, segment names, functional description, calls, methodology-- precede all routines?	☐	☐
Are blank comment lines interspersed throughout the code to make important comments stand out?	☐	☐
Are ample descriptive comments present on instruction lines?	☐	☐
Is tricky coding avoided?	☐	☐
Is addressing of the form "LABEL + 16" avoided?	☐	☐
Does the assembler and/or compiler produce an alphabetized index of labels?	☐	☐
Are all communication areas clearly defined?	☐	☐
Are coding limitations--e.g., limit on the number of instructions--carefully spelled out?	☐	☐
Are program and segment names specified?	☐	☐

NOTES

XI. Testing

A. INTRODUCTION

Careful integration of test procedures into project activities is one of the keys to successful project enactment. From the earliest days of planning, consideration must be given to the means of verification of product quality. Tests themselves must meet those standards applied to the product system.

B. TEST STANDARDS

The two general criteria by which testing procedures are measured are reliability and validity. In considering tests of a programming system, there are additional criteria: completeness, ease of implementation, requirements in terms of resources expended.

Test procedures must be evaluated throughout the project to insure that they:

- Control system quality.

- Comply with the acceptable standards.

The creation of tests is a parallel project, enacted within the programming system project itself. Test specifications are submitted to the same reviewing procedures as product specifications (see Chapter IV, "Specification Reviews"). Test systems are documented as thoroughly as the project product system (see Chapter VIII, "Documentation").

C. DESIGNING THE TEST PROCEDURES

When the proposed system is first specified--i.e., when a PROGRAMMING FUNCTIONAL SPECIFICATION is drawn up--test techniques are planned and designed. Part of the system concept may well be the technique by which it is to be tested.

As some networks have self-checking capabilities built into the circuit design, a similar technique should be included in complex programming network systems. This is especially true of real-time and time-shared operating systems.

D. TEST PROCEDURES AND ANALYSIS

Tests are developed in the same cyclic manner as the program product. The range of complexity of the enactment varies from a simple list of requests to a complex variation of programs.

Additional programs that serve for testing only are specified along with the product programs.

A program which scans a large number of record types, for example, should be tested by means of another program which generates all possible permutations of the record types. Even those test techniques which are not properly speaking program efforts are specified. An information-retrieval system test procedure, for example, might consist of a series of requests for the possible types of information handling. In such a case the documentation of the test results would constitute the major part of the effort.

The test procedure is a component of the overall effort. Including the test component in the design may result in additional special-purpose programs, hardware, or documentation which must be considered in planning. It is possible that testing requirements may require a particular type of system modularization.

1. Planning test requirements.

    While the PROGRAMMING FUNCTIONAL SPECIFICATIONS provide a description of the proposed system in terms of a technical effort, the WORK PLAN shows the system in terms of required resource expenditures. It is extremely important, then, that testing be defined and its extent predicted when the basic estimates are made.

    The programming staff who create the product system are responsible for the quality of their own contributions. A large independent staff might be required to create the test system.

    This test staff may be either programmers or specialists in other fields. For example, a test group checking a statistical cross-tabulation program should include a market researcher or some other expert trained in statistical research.

    It is argued that programmers can create "real life" test situations to use for debugging and thus simulate the actual-use conditions. There are flaws in the argument. A person who has daily contact with a situation--the eventual user class--is certainly more aware of the subtleties of his field, including problem areas. He has the necessary data at hand to set up tests. He has the ability to evaluate results in terms of the context in which the system is used.

    The programmer, on the other hand, rarely possesses a depth of background in the subject area. Inventing test cases is time consuming and costly for him. His interest is in the intricacies of the program.

    Resource utilization can be wasteful in other areas besides programmer time. Before release the product system must be submitted to extensive system testing in simulation of the "live use." Generally, this means much machine time. A programmer can test his own contribution with data of smaller volume. Trying to run large volumes of data through debug shots is costly. Artificial "blowing up" of small test cases to produce volume test cases simply results in running more cases through the same test paths.

172

2. <u>Impact of test resource requirements.</u>

It is evident that a test staff must be included in the early estimates of the project requirements. The size of the staff depends upon the system. The testing of some systems may adequately be done by one qualified individual.

When staffing a project, it might not be feasible to assign independent personnel to the test project. One solution is to use the same staff of programmers to test each other's contributions. The obvious disadvantages of such a situation are:

- A limited viewpoint, resulting from coding the product, which may be carried into the tests.

- Extension of the time element.

- Inadequate competence of individuals performing the tests.

Ideally, the testing staff should be drawn from personnel completely outside the implementing group. A product quality control department responsible for insuring the excellence of all programming products could fulfill this function. If such a group is used, estimates might include research costs into the subject area.

If such a group does not exist, one recourse is to use an outside consulting group. This, too, must be planned early enough so that the selected group can be ready when testing is to begin.

It is advisable for the testers to be the future maintenance staff for a complex system which will require a long period of maintenance.

Good testing may require the addition of special hardware, as well as software, elements. For example, when a remote operation is planned, pseudo transmission equipment might be an effective means of simulating the actual conditions. These requirements are included in the estimates.

3. <u>Debugging.</u>

The staff which creates the product performs its own DEBUGGING function. This may be an individual or group effort. The final presystem debugging stage is performed by the entire group.

In a multimodular system, a module may be introduced with simulated system interfaces. As this module is checked out, additional interacting ones should be added until the complete system has been checked out.

Debugging tasks are documented with the same care as the development activities. Any data-generation programs are flowcharted.

The self-checking technique in debugging is implemented in simple form.
Checkout runs contain:

- Intermediate printout of results.

- Comments of additional output statements.

- Debugging instructions for maintenance.

Similar to the simulation of system interface is the introduction by the
programmer of artificial interfaces within his own program. This permits
checking out of sections of the program at a time. As an example, at a
logical breakpoint in the code, data results may be printed and the program
may be transferred to an exit. At this point the program may accept pseudo
input--the artificially prepared correct results had the previous section run
to successful completion.

Careful documentation and recording of the results of these debugging runs
are essential for the maintenance function. The logical points at which the
program may be broken, as indicated in the documentation, may provide
invaluable service for later modification or for tracking down a malfunction.

Programmed traces and dumps may, of course, be provided in a given
operating system. The use of a systematic dump in cases of abnormal
termination of a checkout run may be valuable. However, carefully
structured debugging runs with maximum intermediate-result display are
preferable. The programmer who thoroughly understands his program
and its relationship to the environment in which it operates is not the
programmer who dumps and puzzles over the result. As debugging documentation, dumps taken in cases of complete lack of knowledge of a situation are valueless.

Test specifications are prepared according to the function and nature of
the product system during the ANALYSIS stage. These specifications may
be of a multilevel variety for programming purposes. In any event they
are submitted to the usual reviewing procedures.

4. Testing flowcharts.

Test programs are flowcharted in the standard manner. Test procedures
which cannot be translated into programs may also be flowcharted if they
lend themselves to pictorialization. FLOWCHARTS, too, are review
documentation.

5. Test programs.

The programming activity which is part of the testing effort is performed
like the product programming. The programming staff makes up specifications and FLOWCHARTS. Program listings are documented. Test
data listings, where applicable, are included. WORK REVIEWS are held
with the group leaders and the programming project leader. WEEKLY
PROGRESS REPORTS are submitted to the programming project leader.

Test programmers need not produce a REFERENCE MANUAL.

Automatic procedures--for example, the sending, receiving, and checking of some message on a periodic basis--can serve to check both a software programming system and the hardware system.

Checkpoints might be included in system design as a means of evaluating results up to a given point. These checkpoints could be periodic measurements of some specific argument against a predicted value for the variable chosen. Actual implementation is, of course, system dependent. In some instances, where programmed checking is not simple, special monitoring or timing hardware devices might be necessary. Checkout of such devices is itself a test procedure.

In simpler systems simple methods can be used. Statistics can be collected during an operation by which the system is later checked. For example, the number of repositionings of an input-output unit required during a run might indicate programming system inefficiency as much as hardware deficiencies.

E. TEST TECHNIQUE IN BASIC DESIGN

Test techniques are incorporated into the PROGRAMMING FUNCTIONAL SPECIFICATION. As the product is conceived, the test procedures that are needed to check it out are also determined.

F. SYSTEM TEST

When all logical parts of the product system have been judged trouble free, they are turned over to the testing group. It is assumed that the tests are ready for implementation. This implies that their capability to perform their function has been demonstrated--i.e., that they are valid; it also implies that their reliability has been judged acceptable.

The system testing group checks the product in an early user situation. All potential situations are simulated; this in essence becomes the first phase of product maintenance.

1. System performance.

System testing is by definition an exhaustive exploration of system facilities. All aspects of system performance are investigated by means of extensive use of its capabilities. The result of the investigation is the clear picture of the actual properties of the finished product and its behavior in all user situations.

2. System conformance.

The performance of the system is an objective appraisal of the functioning of the finished product. How this action relates to the original design and how it fulfills its role in the product line are the subjects of the test system report prepared for the ACCEPTANCE REVIEW.

3. Test documentation.

   The TEST SYSTEM REPORT contains the above-mentioned evaluation as
   formulated by the testing group. It also includes the documented specifications, any FLOWCHARTS, LISTINGS, and a log of test activities.   A
   TEST LOG has an entry for each test showing the characteristic being
   tested, the method, and the results. Special test data prepared for system
   testing are also labeled and presented with the report.

   Judgments of the testers regarding the external characteristics of the
   product are documented as well. Facility of employing the system, ease
   of understanding the conventions, and compatibility with pertinent existing
   contextual or environmental conditions are the items included.

4. System testing under simulation.

   When system testing takes place in whole or in part under simulation, it
   cannot be regarded as conclusive. As soon as possible it must be repeated
   under actual conditions. This could be conceptually impossible. For example, if a transatlantic transmission of input was simulated, the first
   actual use might be "live." Early customer use can, therefore, in such a
   case be considered as an extension of system test. The goal of system
   testing is thorough, exhaustive, sophisticated examination and evaluation
   of advertised system capabilities. Verification of product claims is
   absolutely necessary before release.

5. Self-checking techniques after release.

   Some systems, as described in Item C, above, "Designing the Test Procedures," may have built-in checking facilities. These may be of the
   statistical or diagnostic type. In any case, they give rise to some form
   of output. Wherever these techniques are not costly to the user, they
   should be retained.

G. TESTING AFTER RELEASE

The initial period of customer use is to be regarded as a test period. Test
procedures should be so thorough as to make the incidence of malfunction un-
likely. To insure that the desired quality standards are maintained, the user
should be provided with forms for recording any suspected system error.
Every report must be carefully evaluated and investigated.

Error may result from a misunderstanding of the way in which the system
functions or from conventions of its use. In these cases it is generally the
explanatory documentation that is at fault.

However, a real system malfunction may be detected. Test procedures to
verify the condition should include the simulation of the error-producing run--
i.e., the use of the actual data and retesting using original system test cases.
The difference in the cases used for the system test and the "live data" should
prove indicative of the area in which the problem lies.

After an error has been corrected, the entire system is extensively retested. Even those functions which do not directly depend on the changed section are tested. The new test case is then included in the standard set of system test data to be used for any subsequent verifications.

When a trouble-free use period has been experienced, the testing function as such is completed. During system maintenance, modifications may, of course, be made to the original design. For this period, the original system tests serve as the basic test techniques. Each change to the system adds to the documented test procedures retained for quality assurance.

TEST LOG

SYSTEM NAME:

VERSION NUMBER:

EXTERNAL REFERENCES:

    For example, USASI standards.

TESTING GROUP:

DATE TESTED:

FEATURE TESTED:

    Specify what has been tested. In addition include limitations or external considerations where applicable.

METHOD USED:

    Briefly describe how the feature is tested.

RESULT:

RECOMMENDATION:

    Indicate whether the feature is acceptable, provisionally acceptable with modifications needed, or unacceptable.

LISTING:

    Give the reference number or name.

FLOWCHART REFERENCE NUMBER:

CHECKLIST FOR
TESTING

	YES	NO
Has an independent testing group been formed?	☐	☐
Are testers issued revised REFERENCE MANUALS on a regular basis?	☐	☐
Do they receive prepublication copies of USER MANUALS?	☐	☐
Are specialists in the application field included in the testing group?	☐	☐
Is the testing group large enough?	☐	☐

> GENERALLY SPEAKING, AT LEAST ONE PERSON SHOULD BE ASSIGNED TO QUALITY ASSURANCE FOR EVERY TEN IMPLEMENTERS.

	YES	NO
Has component testing taken place prior to SYSTEM TEST?	☐	☐

Does the TESTING group produce:

	YES	NO
● Weekly and monthly progress reports?	☐	☐
● FLOWCHARTS?	☐	☐
● INTERNAL SYSTEMS descriptions of test programs?	☐	☐
● TEST SPECIFICATIONS?	☐	☐
Is a logic exercisor part of the TEST SYSTEM?	☐	☐
Is this set of programs run every time a change is made to the SYSTEM?	☐	☐

NOTES

XII. Maintenance and Modification

A. INTRODUCTION

The problem of system maintenance and modification varies according to the size and complexity of the programming product in question. Small packages may require only the occasional attention of one of the implementers in response to a user question or bug report; large-scale systems cannot be maintained without a more formal approach. While this chapter is geared to the problem of maintaining a large-scale system, many of the ideas contained in it have more general applicability.

In the sequel, the word "maintenance" takes on a broad meaning. The above title, "Maintenance and Modification," indicates the direction in which the definition is expanded.

B. PLANNING FOR MAINTENANCE

1. The maintenance staff.

During the implementation of the system, the programming staff writes WEEKLY PROGRESS REPORTS, which are sent to the programming project leaders. As programs near completion, these reports include recommendations for the competencies required in the maintenance staff on the basis of programming techniques used. (See Chapter VIII, "Documentation.")

The original programmer--or, at least, a member of his group--is the ideal maintainer of any given program. Assigning all of the original programming staff to the maintenance function is not necessary or desirable for the following reasons:

- A smaller staff is required for maintenance than for program development.

- A given programmer's position in the programming staff structure may change so that he is removed from contact with the original system.

- System maintenance is an ideal introduction to the problem of large-scale system implementation. The job has obvious educational potential.

- The lead programmers are needed elsewhere.

Therefore, a maintenance staff should be selected from programmers who can benefit from contact with the concepts and techniques embodied in the system, as well as from the original programming group. An ideal maintenance group is composed of a few of the original implementers--preferably those with leadership ability--and a selected staff of programmers having the requisite abilities and interests.

181

2. **The task of the project development staff.**

The programming staff, which originates the product system, has three contributions to make to the maintenance activity. These are:

- Defining the most desirable experience level for the individuals chosen to maintain their programs.

- Preparing clear documentation, especially internal systems documentation.

- Advising and assisting in the analysis of early error reports.

The first task of the project staff, indicating desirable areas of competence for the maintainers, is carried out during implementation. The recommendations made are contained in the commentary added to the WEEKLY REPORTS prepared by the programmers. It is the task of the programming project leader to assess the suggestions and send them to the programming manager.

Documentation, the second responsibility, is an ongoing task throughout project development. While all documentation is directed toward communication of system information, the latent character of the need for such materials as INTERNAL SPECIFICATIONS places them in a special relationship to writing standards. The originating programmer bears the added responsibility of diagnosing the ultimate needs of a maintenance staff.

Clarity--the absence of jargon or other contingent terminology--is extremely important. Notes referring to the techniques used should be appended. Motivation underlying choice of method, etc. is a good guide to the final working out of the selected techniques. Wherever applicable, bibliographic information should be provided to give the maintainer the references that will help him simulate the context in which the product with which he is confronted was conceived.

The third task of the originating programmer in assisting a maintainer is that of advising in the assessment of early error reports. This is important for two reasons, based on the intimate knowledge the creator possesses of his work. First, he can readily evaluate any malfunction allegation in terms of his program's action to determine whether it is more likely to be based on a real error or on misunderstanding. In the second place, he can quickly isolate the probable area of trouble.

Whenever possible, the advisory function should be extended to a consulting/teaching activity. Time spent need not be great. The creating programmer along with the maintainer, should go through the exercise of determining both the cause of the error and a feasible solution.

Should the above course prove impractical, some effort should be made to prepare additional guides if the latter are meaningful. For programs which lend themselves to such treatment, cautions or admonitions should be drawn up for the maintainer. The content of these would be simply lists of possible user misunderstandings. Where to look, in a general way, for a given suspected malfunction should be clearly indicated in commentary, narrative descriptions, and flowcharts.

The PROJECT ENACTMENT CHART indicates that the IMPLEMENTER MAINTENANCE phase concludes when the product is accepted by the customer. It is more accurate to say that no implementer leaves the maintenance team until customer acceptance occurs. Beginning at that time, the project leader of the maintenance effort may begin phasing out those personnel not slated to remain with the project. This reduction in staff should take place slowly. No one should leave until his portion of the system is fully understood by his successors.

3. Designing a malfunction report.

A standard form is supplied to the user for reporting any suspected malfunction. Each product system has a report designed to meet its needs. As the enactment progresses, the programming project leader compiles recommendations for the items of information to be included. These items are extracts from the notes and suggestions contained in the WEEKLY REPORTS he receives.

4. The user's role in maintenance.

Clear directions for submitting descriptions of any suspected malfunction are given to the users. Any applicable supporting documentation that is required--program decks, data listings, etc.--are described as well.

Insofar as possible, the user is protected against the chance of further error in developing a corrected system. When corrections are issued, his role in their implementation is limited as much as is consistent with efficiency and reliability. (See the section which discusses implementation of corrections.)

Users are discouraged from making corrections to the system. Sophisticated user groups maintain experienced systems programming staffs which may investigate system action and suggest remedial measures for detected errors. This practice is discouraged for the following reasons:

● Errors are evaluated by the originating project group (see the chapter "Specification Reviews") to determine whether they are real or apparent. Conceivably, a user might misunderstand the system design and find a way to alter it to meet his expectations.

● Even in cases of real error the manner in which a correction is made could have critical implications for planned modifications or errors in other areas. A given user is not aware of the larger context of system use and is, therefore, dependent upon the project staff for information about the feasibility of a given correction.

C. PROCESSING AN ERROR REPORT

1. Recording and verification.

All error reports submitted--even false ones--supply information about the project that may be applied in subsequent similar situations. Reports which describe apparent malfunctions arising from misunderstanding of system use are indicative of one of the following:

- Poor user documentation.

- Inadequate user preparation and training.

- Nonstandard system performance, which caused confusion as to results.

When the primary information has been recorded, a verification is made. This is done in two parts:

- The report itself is investigated thoroughly. If the error is only apparent, the materials are returned, the log entries are completed, and an explanation is provided to the customer.

- Reports which describe those errors not clearly caused by misunderstanding of system use are returned to the maintainer for test processing. The maintenance staff simulates the experience which gave rise to the error. If the error is not duplicated, the user is requested to retry the system and submit his findings. If necessary, the maintenance staff meets with the user to duplicate the original condition in which the error occurred.

2. Testing and documenting corrections.

When a system malfunction has been established, the maintenance programmer makes whatever change is required to correct the error.

- The system is first tested using the submitted materials for the case which uncovered the error.

- Then an exhaustive system test is made to determine whether any other area of performance is affected by the change.

In the process of implementing a change, new listings may be generated. These immediately become the official product documentation. Prior listings--thoroughly annotated--become part of the project archives. Any other affected documentation is corrected as well.

The documentation submitted to substantiate the error report--the test data, etc.--is added to the system test materials. Whenever subsequent tests are made to check overall product performance, the error report tests are included.

3. <u>Issuing changes</u>.

When an error has been corrected, the maintenance log entries are made and the change is incorporated in the next version of the system. All affected user groups* are sent notification of changes and correction materials immediately.

After a period of time, corrections made in response to malfunctions may, because of the urgency of swift response, require cleanup. It is suggested that the system reorganization be made on a monthly basis. The following procedure is suggested:

- Respond to complaints as soon as possible with appropriate interim corrections.

- Make system cleanup a part of your normal day-to-day activity (see Section D, "Modifications") so as better to organize changes that have been made since the last overall revised system was issued.

- Issue an entire new system reflecting the cleanup effort on a monthly basis.

4. <u>Error report statistics</u>.

A series of evaluation reports grow up from the studies of error reports. They are eventually included in CONFORMANCE REPORTS, which provide performance information. The maintenance report log may add a further dimension to such data. Trouble areas can be pinpointed from a study of the errors detected. Simple linear charts of error reports received can be used to watch system action both for present error frequency and in order to predict possible termination of full-scale maintenance. Figure X.2 illustrates a possible format. The total number of error reports and the total number of real errors detected are both plotted against time.

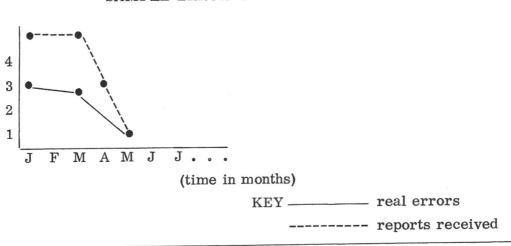

FIGURE X.2
SAMPLE ERROR REPORT CHART

(time in months)

KEY ———————— real errors

- - - - - - - - - reports received

---

*See Section D, on modification, for further discussion of "affected" users.

More detailed statistics can easily be obtained from the same log. A study of errors in specific areas might be set up as shown in Figure X.3, which tabulates real errors against system components.

FIGURE X.3
SAMPLE SYSTEM ERROR CHART

Error Statistics for the Period xx to yy

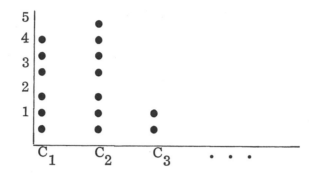

Statistical charts such as these may be used to predict the expected error-report activity. A system which has received extensive use and has been heavily corrected can be regarded as approaching stability. An overall error chart used in conjunction with detailed trouble-area information can serve to indicate which maintainers may be phased out and how many, and the desirable experience for those retained.

D. MODIFICATION

Modifications are made to the system during maintenance, when time allows. They can be proposed by the customer or the maintenance group and can range from the very difficult to the trivial. Most trivial modifications can be classed in the general category of "cleanup." Cleanup is generally thought to be part of the normal day-to-day duties of the maintenance group and requires no particular action by the maintenance project leader. Proposed revisions which entail a significant amount of work must be reviewed and planned for as would any small programming project.

1. Evaluating modification requests.

When modification requests are received, they are evaluated by the programming project leader and the project engineer from the technical viewpoint only. Programmers responsible for the original system or members of the maintenance staff may be consulted to round out details of the technical implications of the request. The programming project leader appends resource estimates, and the entire file is referred to management for decision.

There may be simply a trivial "decision" step in some cases. Products may be developed with modifications anticipated and provided for in original contracts. Or it may be known that resources will be easily obtained or can only be provided with difficulty and delay.

2. Implementing changes.

The status log:

When approval for a modification is given, it is entered in the system status log. Figure X.4 shows headings which might be used in such a log:

FIGURE X.4
SYSTEM STATUS LOG INFORMATION

SYSTEM NAME
PROGRAMMING PROJECT LEADER
GENERAL FEATURES
DATE RELEASED
DATE OF MODIFICATION
NATURE OF MODIFICATION
REQUESTED BY

3. Putting the change into the system.

Wherever possible, a system is conceived of in functional modules which interrelate to perform the overall task. Such a design makes both error correction and modification easier to carry out. A modification is introduced into the system as a new module wherever possible. The new module may be either an addition or a replacement for an already existing one whose action is to be changed.

The programmer making the modification generates new listings and, if necessary, new user documentation pages. New listings become the final reference material for the modified version, once the modified system has been checked out. Such modified listings are clearly identified by being given a version number.

4. Distributing modifications.

Modified systems should be distributed on a monthly basis. It is not advisable (with a large system) to issue changes only as they are made. Changes tend to be issued before they are checked out, and too many versions of the system are generated. This leads to confusion over what version of the system caused which failure to occur, and so forth.

It is always preferable to release a modified system as a whole. This means new listings, FLOWCHARTS where applicable, and replacement or correction pages to user documents wherever necessary. Only when it is clearly more efficient to make a partial release--a single component of a large system, for example--should a partial product release be made.

CHECKLIST FOR
MAINTENANCE AND MODIFICATION

	YES	NO
Have staff members indicated the programming qualifications that should be expected of the maintenance group prior to SYSTEMS TEST?	☐	☐
Is the INTERNAL SYSTEMS MANUAL in a finished form prior to SYSTEMS TEST?	☐	☐
Is it planned that during early release the implementers will take part in maintenance?	☐	☐
Will some members of the project staff remain permanently with the maintenance group?	☐	☐
Are ERROR REPORT statistics kept?	☐	☐

Is there a system for field reporting on:

	YES	NO
● Software malfunction?	☐	☐
● Software mismatch to documentation?	☐	☐
● Software performance?	☐	☐
● Nonconformity to standards?	☐	☐
Is the reporting system documented?	☐	☐

Is this documentation available to:

	YES	NO
● Software and maintenance personnel?	☐	☐
● User representatives?	☐	☐
● Users?	☐	☐
Is maintenance turnaround optimized by the use of high-speed communications systems?	☐	☐
If corrections cannot be made immediately, does there exist a reporting scheme that will keep the customer informed of progress?	☐	☐
Are corrections consolidated on a monthly basis, and is a new system distributed monthly?	☐	☐

NOTES

NOTES

XIII. Personnel Selection

A. INTRODUCTION

Personnel of a large company are hired by the employment office. This office screens prospective applicants, preinterviews them to insure that they meet corporate standards in personnel selection, and handles the general administrative work which must accompany the application of a prospective candidate for a job in the programming department. Of course, this organization also performs other vital services in orienting personnel to the company, handling personnel problems, etc.

The reader may be asked to interview prospective employees in order to ascertain whether or not they will be suitable to perform specific tasks in his area. This chapter discusses techniques in interviewing these candidates which one might want to use in fulfilling the requirements of that task.

It should be remembered that common sense, first and foremost, is the best "tool" in interviewing candidates. Just as the candidate is representing himself to the interviewer, so the interviewer is representing the company to the candidate. Thus whether or not the prospective employee is offered a job and/or accepts a job, it is important that he be treated with the utmost courtesy. This, of course, goes without saying. It is mentioned because personnel who may be called upon to interview a prospective employee but who have not had experience in interviewing before may not realize that the person being interviewed is, in addition to being a candidate for a job, a potential source of unfair criticism of the environment to others who may be considering joining the company--or, alternatively, a source of encouragement to others to apply. Thus starting with a realization of the need for common sense and courtesy, the interview (and this chapter) may proceed.

Assume that you have been called upon to aid the employment office in providing your opinion of the value of a particular candidate's background in your highly specialized technical area. The next sections suggest methods by which you can discharge this responsibility.

B. A SET OF GENERAL RULES

1. After meeting the candidate, take him to the area in which you plan to interview him and insure that he is put at ease.

2. Do not make the interview seem like an inquisition. It is better that you start your technical questioning after having exchanged a few pleasant remarks concerning some topic other than that which you intend to interview the candidate upon. For example, you might discuss his trip to the company, a recent event in the computer field, or any other (usually, noncontroversial) topic which seems reasonable.

3. Remember, no matter what your own personal disposition may be during the day you are interviewing the candidate, do not make disparaging

remarks about your job, your associates, the company, etc. Doing so will insure that the candidate will think very little of you, as well as, perhaps of the company. This is pointed out here because sometimes the interviewer may have the tendency to feel that such remarks are understood to be representative of a bit of playfulness or may be used to inject a bit of humor into the interview. Unfortunately, they are almost never taken in that vein.

4. Your interview may be considered to be in three parts:

- The "hello" sequence.

- The question period--wherein the candidate should expound quite freely upon what he is capable of doing, what he likes to do, what he wants to do, what he can do, etc. In this part the candidate should do most of the talking.

- The interviewer part, where the candidate listens to either a polite "sales pitch" or a polite termination of the interview.

As indicated above, in Part 2 the candidate is supposed to do most of the talking. This, of course, will not be the case if the candidate is known to be wanted by the company and his employment is guaranteed should he accept. In that case, of course, you must be a salesman for the position which the company would like to fill with the candidate's services.

5. Whatever you do, do not inadvertently misrepresent either the job or the company. Remember, should this occur and should the candidate accept, you may have great difficulty after his arrival.

6. If you feel that the candidate is desirable but he requires more "convincing" then you personally may be able to give in his particular case, do not hesitate to call in others to help out.

7. Remember that in addition to any technical competencies the person may have, other qualities are necessary for effective performance within the company. These are, of course, the capability to get along with others, awareness of the normal courtesies which one would expect from a fellow employee, a sense of dedication to his job, etc. To hire solely on technical capability is in the long run a great error.

8. If you see any signs of nonacceptable past behavior--exhibited by the candidate on past jobs--there is a high probability that he has not changed. Thus, for example, should the candidate tell you of a clever trick played on a previous employer for whom he worked, you run a great risk in hiring him. Sometimes an interviewer not professionally trained in this area will forget that evidence of past behavior problems frequently signifies future ones too.

9. The candidate must, of course, be viewed in many ways with regard to the specific technical job for which you may be interviewing him. For example, working in a group may not be his forte or, conversely, he may be unable to work alone. This may not show up if one merely concerns himself with the technical aspects of the interview.

10. One very important factor frequently forgotten in ascertaining the desirability of a candidate is whether the interviewer "likes" him or not. Remember, no matter what the evidence of performance may be in the past on the part of the candidate, if you don't like him during the interview <u>you probably won't after</u> you recommend his hiring and he shows up on the job. Also, <u>what is commonly not known is that feelings of dislike toward</u> an individual are, in the large majority of cases, not hidable. A companion rule is that if A dislikes B, B probably dislikes A. Much success in job performance depends upon feelings of goodwill between the people working together.

The rules given above are but a small set of the many which professional interviewers know. They should be considered by the technical staff member aiding the employment office interviewer. Some deal with the psychological aspects of the interview; others, with protocol. Whatever the case, they are highly relevant.

The following section is a general discussion of other aspects of candidate interviewing.

C. OTHER CONSIDERATIONS

While it is not expected that personnel who have not been trained in professional interviewing would know the fine points of this activity, <u>some things are expected just by virtue of the fact</u> that the company places some of its faith and judgment in the hands of the interviewer. Some awareness should be had by the interviewer of the problems which a candidate may have in being interviewed. For example, some candidates may be very good at verbalizing upon a wide variety of topics; however, they may be quite poor in taking a written examination. Of course, the opposite case exists also, as do various degrees between these two extremes.

Also, many candidates are highly nervous upon being interviewed for a position, and this nervousness may take various forms. The interviewer can, by virtue of recognizing this fact, help the candidate to overcome it by merely a few words of encouragement. On the other hand, great self-assurance, if recognized to be unjustified in the candidate's case, is in the same way frequently a manifestation of the candidate's fear during the interview. The interviewer may decide that the candidate is bragging, when this really need not be the case. Some sort of psychological insight must be practiced by the successful interviewer.

One other very important point which is frequently overlooked during an interview is the determination of whether the prospective candidate has a <u>sense of humor</u>. This is not to say that he must be a virtual well of jokes and/or foolishness, for this is not desirable. Rather, his sense of humor must be tested, because the pressures of the programming job are such that without it a man may not perform properly. One method of ascertaining whether the person has a sense of humor is to ask very candidly whether he thinks there is anything about his work habits or personal disposition which at times might be considered laughable. If he cannot find anything about himself which borders at least upon being generally accepted as humorous, the probability is that he is a difficult person to get along with. Of course, <u>asking such a question must be done with goodwill on the part of the interviewer and with much tact.</u> Some candidates for employment betray the fact that they will be very hard to get along with by considering the work around them completely in need of correction and their own role in it to be that of corrector. Thus the foregoing consideration is but one element of the interviewer's concern; however, it turns out that given all things equal, the candidate with a well-regulated sense of humor is more desirable to acquire than the competing candidate who is nothing but dead earnest.

Summing up, there are three attributes which you must look for in each candidate who is applying for a position working in your area. The following questions must be answered:

- Does he fit into the group?

- Does he appear bright and capable of learning (consistent with the demands of the job)?

- Does he have experience in the technical aspects of the job?

Note the order in which these three attributes are given. Reversing them is frequently an error. Of course, the particular job in question may cause one or another of these attributes to be of greatest importance; however, if a group effort is involved, attribute number one should be considered most important.

This section is followed by a "Notes" section (as are all sections in the book). You may want to keep records of how your interviews of candidates went, what was said, etc. for future reference. It should be clear that the technical demands of successful interviewing are as complex as may be found in any other discipline. To assume increasing job responsibilities within your own career, you will have to become proficient in this area.

NOTES

Appendix

APPENDIX 1

HOW TO USE THE MODEL REPORTS

Some sections of this book use model reports as a guide in writing PROJECT REPORTS. One such model exists in this Appendix.

Before actually beginning to generate a document from a model, read the introductory material in the relevant chapter. In so doing you will learn how the production of the document should relate to the effort in general, and in addition you will be advised of the audience for which you are writing.

Keep in mind that:

- The reports must be written in terms familiar to management personnel.

- "In" words and jargon should be avoided.

- The terms you use must be defined in a <u>GLOSSARY OF TERMS</u>.

The basic rules that have been followed in the models are discussed below:

- Use the headings, except when they are not applicable or when a change can make them more meaningful.

- These headings represent the general categories of information that should be covered in the document.

- Do not discard a heading without giving it careful consideration.

- Deletion of a topic could lead to the exclusion of an important block of information.

Whether or not you use all the suggested headings, create your own subheadings whenever you must discuss two or more minor topics under the same topic.

Make sure that your subheadings are clear; there must be no question in the reader's mind as to what you will discuss under each.

The model makes use of the following conventions:

- Major topic headings appear in upper case type and are underlined.

- Suggested subheadings appearing in PART II are capitalized but not underlined.

- Explanatory text is in upper and lower case Roman type.

WORK PLAN MODEL

project name

WORK PLAN

date

TABLE OF CONTENTS

I. INTRODUCTION

Briefly state the sequence of events that led to the production of the document. Describe its content and define how best to use it. If unusual ATTACHMENTS appear, explain their relevance.

In a separate paragraph outline your understanding of the limits of your project responsibility.

This section need not vary in revised versions of the document.

II. ACTIVITIES TO BE PERFORMED

A. THE EFFORT WILL FALL INTO THE FOLLOWING CATEGORIES:

1. DEVELOPMENT OF NEW COMPUTER PROGRAMS
2. MODIFICATION OF EXISTING COMPUTER PROGRAMS
3. VERIFICATION OF EXISTING COMPUTER PROGRAMS
4. DEVELOPMENT OF DOCUMENTATION
5. MAINTENANCE OF COMPUTER PROGRAMS

The intention of this section is to characterize the task by identifying the types of activities to be performed. The above list does not represent all possibilities or an acceptable minimum classification; it is a suggestion only.*

Item 5 is very important. Some system components depend on the existence of a working version of other programs in the system. It must be recognized that such dependencies force the maintenance of "primary programs" before SYSTEM TEST begins.

B. COMMENTS REGARDING ACTIVITIES TO BE PERFORMED PER MODULE

Discuss particular components of the job that require any unusual activities.

C. SPECIFICATION OF THE ACTIVITIES TO BE PERFORMED PER SYSTEM COMPONENT

Unless the number of system components and the number of activity classifications are quite small, this section should be a reference to an ATTACHMENT. The most effective means of presenting this information is by chart. List activity types (A_j) horizontally and system components (C_i) vertically. If C_i requires the performance of A_j, indicate this by an X in the ith row and jth column. If not, leave the cell blank.

See sample ATTACHMENT 1.

---

*Reference CHART 1-A (see Supplement 1, Chapter II, "Work Plan Preparation") for a complete breakdown of all activities. This chart should appear in an attachment.

III. STAFFING PATTERN

A. DISCUSSION

Reference CHARTS 1-B and 3 (see Supplement 1, Chapter II, "Work Plan Preparation") and discuss attributes of each.

B. ASSUMPTIONS

List the assumptions under which the personnel estimates have been made. It is normal to assume, for example, a given time period and a level of ability on the part of the staff. If not all staff members are known, mention this.

C. DEVELOPMENT CONSIDERATIONS

Note the impact of development constraints on the STAFFING PATTERN. Typical considerations are:

- Optimum number of people required per module.

- Time required per module.

- Relations between modules (reference the project network).

D. FLEXIBILITY

Describe the degree to which the staffing pattern can be modified in case of equipment or software delays.

IV. FACILITIES REQUIRED

A. HOUSING FOR THE STAFF

1. TECHNICAL

Estimate the amount of office space required. Note the impact on production if the staff is not seated in the same area.

2. SECRETARIAL

Estimate the amount of typing help required, and list the equipment--typewriter, reproducers, collating machines, etc.--that they will need.

B. OTHER SUPPORT PERSONNEL

Define the number of other support personnel needed. The most urgent requirement will be for typists and secretaries. Support personnel are those who do not take part in the development effort but provide services to those who do; computer operations staff, messengers, and draftsmen are all examples of other support personnel. Reference CHART 1-C (see Supplement 1, Chapter II, "Work Plan Preparation").

C. COMPUTER REQUIREMENTS

1. TIMETABLE

Estimate the computer time need in hours, and present a table of usage per month. Do not neglect to include the SYSTEM TEST requirement as well as that of the DEBUG PHASE. Estimate the impact on the projected completion date of late equipment delivery.*

2. CONFIGURATION

List the minimum machine configuration needed to check out the system.

D. SOFTWARE REQUIREMENTS

List the elements of software, including simulators, that must be operational in order for testing to take place.

Estimate the impact of late software delivery on the projected delivery date of the system.

V. TARGET DATES

List the significant project milestones and the dates at which they are expected to appear. The following should be included.**

PROGRAMMING FUNCTIONAL SPECIFICATION (SYSTEM)
PROGRAMMING FUNCTIONAL SPECIFICATION (PER MODULE)
REFERENCE MANUALS (PER MODULE)
TEST SPECIFICATION
INTERNAL SYSTEMS SPECIFICATION (C)
INTERNAL SYSTEMS SPECIFICATION (B)
INTERNAL SYSTEMS SPECIFICATION (A)
FINAL WORK PLAN
FLOWCHARTS (C)
FLOWCHARTS (B)
FLOWCHARTS (A)

---

*Reference CHARTS 4 and 5 (see Supplement 1, Chapter II, "Work Plan Preparation").

**When an updated version of the WORK PLAN is issued, some of these objects will have already made their appearance. They should be listed, nevertheless, for completeness.

BEGIN SYSTEM TEST
COMPLETE SYSTEM TEST
INTERNAL SYSTEM MANUAL
RELEASE USER DOCUMENTATION
RELEASE FOR CUSTOMER USE
BEGIN EXTERNAL MAINTENANCE

VI. PROJECT NETWORK

A project network is a PERT DIAGRAM representing every component of
the system. Since this chart can be of considerable bulk, it is recommended that it be included as an attachment. This section should consist
of a few remarks on the network and a cross reference to it.

VII. DISCUSSION

Outline the knowledge upon which the content of the WORK PLAN is based.
If sufficient evidence is lacking for precise estimation in some areas,
point this out.

VIII. CONCLUSION

Relate the findings of this document to known management expectations.

ATTACHMENT 1

ACTIVITIES TO BE PERFORMED

PER SYSTEM COMPONENT

The attachments are included to accommodate two possibilities. First, it may
be that the standard topics are not sufficiently general to cover some special
point of interest for the project; additional discussion should then be attached
to the document. Second, some of the standard headings require charts that
are too bulky to include with the text. The PROJECT NETWORK is a typical
example. All foldouts should be appended as ATTACHMENTS to make the
WORK PLAN more readable.

An ATTACHMENT is a cover page--of which this is an example--followed by
the chart or document being included. Since the character of an ATTACHMENT
can vary widely, no attempt is made to specify a particular form for one.

ACTIVITIES TO BE PERFORMED
PER SYSTEM COMPONENT

	$TASK_1$	$TASK_2$	$TASK_3$	$TASK_4$	$TASK_5$	$TASK_6$	.	.	.	$TASK_K$
COMPONENT$_1$	X	X	X		X		.	.	.	X
COMPONENT$_2$	X	X	X		X		.	.	.	
COMPONENT$_3$	X		X	X		X	.	.	.	X
COMPONENT$_4$		X	X	X						
COMPONENT$_5$			X	X		X				X
COMPONENT$_6$	X	X			X	X	.	.	.	
.		X	X		X	X	.	.	.	X
.	X	X	X	X						
.	X	.	X	X		X	.	.	.	X
.		X			X	X				X
.	X	X	X	X	X	X				X
COMPONENT$_N$	X	X		X	X		.	.	.	X

ATTACHMENT 2

CHARTS 1-A, 1-B, 1-C

CHARTS 2, 3, 4, 5

See Supplement 1, Chapter 11, "Work Plan Preparation."

GLOSSARY OF TERMS

Define all technical and unusual terminology used in the text.

Glossary

GLOSSARY

This is not intended to be a general computer word/term glossary. It contains words and terms which need definition for the following reasons:

1. Their meaning (hence usage) may be peculiar to this book.

2. There is no industrywide agreement on their meaning.

GLOSSARY

ACCEPTANCE REVIEW--the review that takes place at the successful completion of SYSTEM TEST. The reviewers study the results of the testing and system testing as well as the documents prepared by the programming staff. If errors or inadequacies are found, additional modification must be made and then a new ACCEPTANCE REVIEW takes place. See Chapter IV, "Specification Reviews."

ACTIVITY--A component part of a project. Design, coding, typing, and attendance at meetings are all examples of activities.

ACTIVITY TO BE PERFORMED--That effort performed between the START-POINT and END-POINT OF A PROJECT, including: flowcharting and analysis, computer coding, computer program check-out, documentation, administrative and clerical work.

ALPHA REVIEW--The review that takes place upon the completion of the PROGRAMMING FUNCTIONAL SPECIFICATION and the WORK PLAN. The project engineer, the programming manager, the section leader, and the programming project leader review these documents. If it is determined that the product has not been satisfactorily understood, the PROGRAMMING FUNCTIONAL SPECIFICATION is rewritten and the review is reinitiated. If the WORK PLAN calls for expenditures in excess of those expected, functions may be cut or the project canceled.

ALPHA REVIEW CONFORMANCE REPORT--The findings of the ALPHA REVIEW COMMITTEE. See Chapter IV, "Specification Reviews."

ANALYSIS--Preliminary phase of project enactment concerned with the problem definition and the establishment of feasibility for the proposed project.

ASA STANDARD GRAPHICS--A graphic representation of computer program logic utilizing illustrative symbols. See Chapter IX, "Flowcharting."

BETA REVIEW--Review intended to insure that design implementation is proceeding in compliance with technical specifications and standards. This activity takes place upon completion of the DESIGN PHASE. See Chapter IV, "Specification Reviews."

CHECKPOINT--See Chapter V, "Project Enactment Checkpoints."

CODING--An ordered list of instructions in machine, assembler, or compiler language form, or the activity required to produce such a list.

COMPONENT--A logically independent subset of a programming system. "Module," "component," and "element" are used interchangeably in the text.

COMPUTER REQUIREMENTS--Estimate of the computer time needed to enact the project; it includes the DEBUG PHASE and the SYSTEM TEST PHASE requirements.

CONFORMANCE REPORT--A report issued by a review committee commenting on the degree to which the proposed product agrees with expectation. See Chapter IV, "Specification Reviews."

CONNECTORS--Linkage lines between related processes described on a FLOWCHART. See Chapter IX, "Flowcharting."

DEBUG--Checkout at the COMPONENT level.

DECISION GROUP--Statements, grouped together for flowcharting purposes, which are associated with a decision or alternative exits. See Chapter IX, "Flowcharting."

DECISION TABLE--A tabular array that relates program decision rules to program actions. See Chapter IX, "Flowcharting."

DESIGN--Preparation for the CODING PHASE. The derivation of techniques to be employed in the final product.

DOCUMENTATION--Descriptive material produced by the programmers and/or technical writers during project enactment. This includes all REPORTS, SPECIFICATIONS, FLOWCHARTS, LISTINGS, and REFERENCE MANUALS.

ELEMENT--A logically independent subset of a programming system. "Module," "component," and "element" are used interchangeably in the text.

END-POINT--Explicit statement of the criteria by which the project will be judged complete. See Chapter III, "Time and Cost Estimating."

ERROR REPORT--See MALFUNCTION REPORT.

EXTERNAL FUNCTIONAL SPECIFICATION--Functional description of a proposed system submitted by an external agency. A work request.

FCFT--See FIXED COST FIXED TIME ESTIMATE.

FIXED COST FIXED TIME ESTIMATE--An estimate of the time and cost of a computer programming project based on complete information--i.e., no significant project enactment parameter is unknown.

FLOWCHARTS--Graphic documentation presenting the analysis of the program in logical steps.

GAMMA REVIEW The review that occurs soon after the beta review. It considers the project status to date and the revised planning documentation. See Chapter IV, "Specification Reviews."

GLOBAL DESCRIPTIVE NAME--An identifier used by more than one component of the system.

GROUP LEADER--A senior PROGRAMMER assigned some management responsibility within a PROGRAMMING GROUP.

HOUSING FACILITIES--The physical office space and furniture necessary for the enactment of a project as specified in the WORK PLAN. See Chapter II, "Work Plan Preparation."

IDENTIFYING LABEL--See LABEL.

INTERNAL SYSTEMS SPECIFICATIONS--A formalization of the purpose, techniques, restrictions, requirements, and rules of the given product. See Chapter V, "Project Enactment Checkpoints."

JOB--Programming assignment.

LABEL--An identifier used to identify a program instruction, command, variable, constant, or area.

LISTINGS--Printed record reflecting the current state of the coding. Valid only until a new assembly or compilation is made; then destroyed. Used to note corrections and results of check runs. The final version is used as a reference for maintenance. It serves as a cross reference to the FLOW-CHARTS through comments. See Chapter IX, "Flowcharting"; Chapter X, "Coding."

LOCAL DESCRIPTIVE NAME--An identifier used internally by some system component.

LOCATION POINT--A point within a sequence of coded instructions.

LOGIC EXERCISOR--A program or set of programs designed to test a software system functionally. This test sequence should be executed every time a MODIFICATION is made.

MAINTENANCE--The act of correcting errors detected in existing programming systems. See Chapter XII, "Maintenance and Modification."

MAINTENANCE LOG--A record of all ERROR REPORTS made during a MAINTENANCE Period.

MALFUNCTION REPORT--A report issued by the user describing some error thought to be caused by a supplied program.

MODIFICATION--A correction made to a program or programs during MAINTENANCE.

MODULE--A logically independent subset of a programming system. "Module," "component," and "element" are used interchangeably in the text.

MONTHLY REPORT--A report originated by the programming project leader and sent to higher management. It contains all the progress effected that month, plus anticipated progress for the coming month. It includes the PROJECT HISTORICAL RECORD. See Chapter VI, "Progress Reporting."

NARRATIVE FLOWCHART--A graphic representation of computer program logic in sentence/paragraph form.

OFFPAGE CONNECTOR--A connector which refers to a logical step on another page in the NARRATIVE FLOWCHART. See CONNECTORS.

OPERATOR'S REFERENCE--That part of the REFERENCE MANUAL directed toward operations personnel. See REFERENCE MANUAL.

OVERALL SYSTEMS MANUAL--That portion of the INTERNAL SYSTEMS MANUAL concerned with the SYSTEM itself, not its various parts. This section includes definitions of all system areas, symbols, tables, and the like.

PERT--A method of controlling and analyzing a project using periodic reports to determine overall status.

PERT DIAGRAM--See PERT NETWORK.

PERT NETWORK--A graphic representation of a project, showing the time relationship and dependencies between tasks to be performed.

PROGRAMMER--Developer of computer programs.

PROGRAMMER'S MANUAL--That part of the REFERENCE MANUAL directed toward programming personnel. See REFERENCE MANUAL.

PROGRAMMING FUNCTIONAL SPECIFICATION--First attempt to formalize the external requirements in terms of the function of the problem. This is drawn up by the programming staff under the direction of the programming project leader.

PROGRAMMING GROUP--A number of PROGRAMMERS and GROUP LEADERS, under the direction of a PROGRAMMING PROJECT LEADER, engaged in a PROGRAMMING PROJECT.

PROGRAMMING MANAGER--Director of the programming organization.

PROGRAMMING PROJECT LEADER--Manager of a PROGRAMMING GROUP.

PROGRESS REPORT--A report stating current status of a job or project. On the programmer level the progress report is called the WEEKLY REPORT. Two higher-level PROGRESS REPORTS are issued by the programming project leader: the PROJECT WEEKLY REPORT and the PROJECT MONTHLY RE-PORT. See Chapter VI, "Progress Reporting."

PROJECT--That group of activities performed between the START-POINT and END-POINT. See Chapter III, "Time and Cost Estimating."

PROJECT ENACTMENT CHART--A flow diagram depicting project development.

PROJECT END-POINT--Point at which prearranged completion criteria for a programming project are satisfied.

PROJECT HISTORICAL RECORD--A charted record of progress in terms of system components. All the past weeks' progress reports are reflected, showing the accomplishments on a weekly basis. A cross-reference document for all progress reports.

PROJECT START-POINT--Point at which the DESIGN PHASE begins. See Chapter III, "Time and Cost Estimating," and Chapter II, "Work Plan Preparation."

PROPOSED CHANGE FORM--A form to be submitted by a PROGRAMMER to his PROGRAMMING PROJECT LEADER requesting that some globally referenced system parameter or area be modified.

REFERENCE MANUAL--Document written by the programmer to describe completely the product he has created. It is used as a reference for programmers preparing test procedures and is source material for the documentation staff producing user documents. It consists of an operations section and a programming section.

SECTION SUPERVISOR-- Leader in charge of a source area of effort within the department--i.e., OPERATING SYSTEMS. The SECTION SUPERVISOR reports directly to the PROGRAMMING MANAGER.

SOFTWARE REQUIREMENTS--A list of those elements of software which must be operational in order to test a given product. This appears in the WORK PLAN.

SPECIFICATION LEVEL--INTERNAL SYSTEMS SPECIFICATIONS and FLOW-CHARTS are produced in graduated levels of completeness. The C-level document appears following DESIGN, B-level appears following CODING, and the A-level appears before CUSTOMER RELEASE. See Chapter V, "Project Enactment Checkpoints."

STAFFING PATTERN--A plan of personnel utilization over the period of the project enactment, specified in the WORK PLAN. See WORK PLAN.

START-POINT--See PROJECT START-POINT.

STATEMENT IDENTIFIER--A unique numeric identifier assigned to a logical step in a NARRATIVE FLOWCHART which is referenced by an OFFPAGE CONNECTOR.

SUBPRODUCT--A document, listing, computer program, or report slated to appear before project completion. See Chapter V, "Project Enactment Check-points."

SUPPORT PERSONNEL--Personnel who do not actually take part in the de-velopment effort but who provide services to those who do.

SYSTEM STATUS LOG--A record of all modifications made during a MAIN-TENANCE period.

SYSTEM TEST--A project enactment phase which tests the entire system once it has been successfully integrated.

TEST--Integrated checkout at the system level.

TEST LOG--A record of tests made by the testing group, showing the feature being tested, the method, and the results. See Chapter XI, "Testing."

TEST PROGRAMS--A set of routines designed to exercise a system fully be-fore its release to the field.

TEST SPECIFICATIONS--An extensive set of procedure definitions for product testing. These specifications are prepared during the ANALYSIS PHASE of the project by an independent group. See Chapter XI, "Testing."

TEST SYSTEM REPORT--Report submitted by the testing group, indicating results and evaluations of the tested product, which is used by those participating in the ACCEPTANCE REVIEW. It includes SPECIFICATIONS, FLOW-CHARTS, LISTINGS, and a log of test activities. See Chapter XI, "Testing."

TIME AND COST ESTIMATE--Report containing the total time, total staff, total cost/work element, project computer time requirement, and the facility requirement for a programming project.

TIME AND MATERIALS ESTIMATE--An estimate of the time and cost of a proposed computer programming project where certain important project enactment parameters are assumed rather than known. A best guess based on incomplete information.

USER MANUALS--User documentation developed by the technical writing group for the potential user. An OPERATIONS MANUAL and the PROGRAMMING MANUAL. See Chapter VIII, "Documentation."

WEEKLY PROJECT REPORT--A report including the current status, the work completed during the current week, anticipated progress for the next week, cause of any slippage, and anticipated problem areas--plus suggested remedies, if any. A summary of all the WEEKLY REPORTS submitted to the programming project leader. See Chapter VI, "Progress Reporting."

WEEKLY REPORT--Progress report form filled in weekly by all programmers.

WORK PLAN--A collection of resource requirement estimates. This includes the activities to be performed, the staffing pattern, the facilities required, a description of the product, target dates, and the project network. It is written in terms familiar to the management personnel. See Chapter II, "Work Plan Preparation."